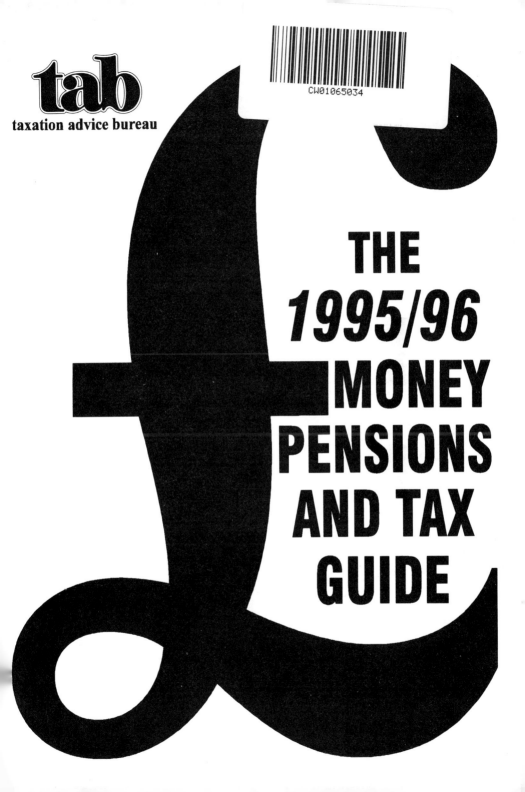

tab
taxation advice bureau

CW01065034

THE
1995/96
MONEY
PENSIONS
AND TAX
GUIDE

This book has been prepared as a general guide for use in the UK and is based on our understanding of present law and practice.

While every effort has been made to ensure accuracy, neither the publisher nor editor is liable for any errors or omissions.

ISBN No.1-897780-86-9

Tax forms reproduced in this book are Crown copyright and are printed with the permission of the Controller of H.M. Stationery Office.

Published By:
The Publishing Corporation UK Ltd.,
Colson House,
Knight Street,
South Woodham Ferrers,
Essex CM3 5ZL.

Printed By:
Redwood Books Ltd.,
Kennet House,
Kennet Way, Trowbridge,
Wiltshire, BA14 8RN.

AUTHOR'S NOTE

Financial and tax affairs are a source of worry to many and attempts to unravel their intricacies are often fraught with difficulty. With the proper use of our Money Pensions & Tax Guide this need no longer be so. However, I would stress that it is intended as a guide and not as a panacea. So, if after reading it, you continue to have difficulty, I would recommened that you seek professional advice.

Sebastian Devlin

16th January 1995

CONTENTS

Part One - Money and Tax Planning

Part Two - Pensions

Part Three - The Tax System

Part Four - Completing Your Annual Tax Return

THE MONEY PENSIONS & TAX GUIDE

This guide is written for the lay person, rather than the taxation or financial specialist. We hope that it will enable you to find solutions to your individual money and tax problems. It will also help you to understand more clearly how our tax and financial system actually work. To facilitate this, the guide is divided into four parts:

PART ONE: Money and Tax Planning

To a surprisingly large extent, it is up to you how well you save or borrow and how much tax you pay. Some methods of raising money will cost you more in financial and tax terms than others. So, it is very important that you understand what your best options are. In this part of the guide, we detail the various options open to you in planning your finances.

PART TWO: Pensions

In this section we outline your pension benefits under three broad headings:

National Insurance Pensions

Employee Pensions

Personal Pensions

PART THREE: The Workings of the Tax System

This section contains a general guide to the UK Tax Code. It gives an accurate guide to the PAYE system and how best to make it work for you. It also includes advice on making your will.

PART FOUR: Completing Your Tax Return

This section lists various documents which you may require before filling in your tax return. It also includes a step by step guide to completing your annual return and outlines exactly what your tax inspector needs to know about you. Full examples are given, thus enabling you to gain optimum benefit from each section.

Whatever your situation - Self-Employed, PAYE or unemployed, this guide will prove itself to be invaluable.

TAB

"The future is like heaven - everyone exalts it, but no one wants to go there now."

James Baldwin

PART ONE

MONEY AND TAX PLANNING

Everybody should know about money and tax planning.
In the following pages, we give you a broad guide to saving and investing, borrowing and providing for family needs in a cost-effective way.

SAVING & INVESTING

A hole in the ground is no place for savings, as it is neither profitable, secure nor tax-efficient. Nowadays, there is a variety of quite cleverly-designed mechanisms to both maximise your returns and minimise your tax liability. Indeed, there is such a wide range of options available that it is necessary to seek out a plan for yourself in order to be sure of selecting the one best-suited to your needs.

The time factor is crucial in any investment plan and you must look ahead. For instance, will you be saving for less than five years or more than five years, for less than ten years or more than ten years?

"The higher the risk, the greater the return", is another guideline. You can decide how much you would like to make and just how much risk you are prepared to take. There is also another aspect to risk: if you commit yourself to saving for five years in regular instalments - what will happen, if for any reason, you find yourself unable to meet the instalments?

Inflation is another factor to be taken into account and the degree to which it might affect the real value of the return which you will eventually receive. To put it in simple terms, the rate of interest you are getting should always exceed the percentage increase in the rate of inflation, so, the trick is to choose either index-linked schemes or schemes that offer a genuinely good return.

Then there is the real bogey - Tax. Since Governments are likely to continue to penalise saving, it is important to settle on a scheme that offers both a handsome return and a tax-efficient way of earning it.

Remember, under independent taxation everybody has a personal allowance. So, everybody can earn up to £3,525 in the 1995/96 tax year without paying income tax. Children have the same basic personal allowances as adults.

A word of warning for parents! If you give your savings as a gift to your children, you may be liable to pay tax on any income generated by these savings, unless your children are over eighteen or married. This will not apply to gifts from grandparents or relatives.

NATIONAL SAVINGS SCHEMES

NATIONAL SAVINGS BANK

The National Savings Bank is operated by the Post Office and guaranteed by the Crown. Anybody over seven years of age can open a National Savings Bank Account. There are two types of account available, an ordinary account and an investment account:

Ordinary Account

You can invest in an ordinary account at most post offices. The minimum investment is £10 and the maximum investment is £10,000, plus accumulated interest. Withdrawals of up to £100 per day may be made on demand.

Two rates of interest are payable. The standard rate is 2% p.a. and the higher rate is 3.25% p.a. To get the higher rate you need to have your account open for a full calendar year e.g. 31st December 1993 to 1st January 1995.

Investment Account

You can start off with a minimum investment of £20 and build this up to a maximum investment of £100,000, plus accumulated interest. The rate of interest is competitive (average 5.75% p.a.) and is paid from the day funds are deposited until the day prior to withdrawal. Interest earned is credited to your account at 31st December each year.

Tax

Interest is paid gross and is taxable. However, the first £70 p.a. on the ordinary account is tax free.

CHILDREN'S BONUS BONDS

Children's bonus bonds are available from July 1991 to under 16's. The minimum holding is £25, which can be increased by multiples of £25, up to a maximum of £1,000, and held until the holder is 21. Interest at date of publication was 7.85% p.a. over five years and it is exempt from tax. Children's bonus bonds are particularly suitable for parents making gifts to their children as no income tax liability will arise to the parents on the interest earned.

National Savings.
Security has never been
so interesting.

All too often these days, someone
shouts "investment opportunity!", and
fools rush in. Thus proving that it's not
always a case of safety in numbers.

The smart money, however, heads for
National Savings to discover an exciting
array of investment opportunities, thought-
fully designed to suit individual needs.

And all with the lifebelt security
you'd expect from National Savings.

So phone us on 0645 645 000
between 9am and 4.30pm Monday to Friday.
(The call will be charged at your local rate)

If you're safety conscious, you won't find
a better way to keep your head above water.

SAVING CERTIFICATES

You can hold up to £10,000 in the 42nd issue. However, if you are reinvesting from earlier certificates held for at least 5 years, or from a yearly plan where certificates were held for at least four years, the £10,000 limit may be increased to a maximum of £30,000. Saving certificates are available in most post offices and many banks. Over a five-year period, the average return is 5.85% p.a. If you encash them early, the return is less and is payable only for each complete period of three months for which the certificates were held.

SAVING CERTIFICATES INTEREST RATES - 42ND ISSUE

	Interest Payable
Year 1	4.00% p.a.
Year 2	4.60% p.a.
Year 3	5.50% p.a.
Year 4	6.75% p.a.
Year 5	8.46 % p.a.

No interest is earned on certificates repaid in the first year, except for 'reinvestment' certificates.

YEARLY PLAN

To avail of this plan, you deposit by standing order a fixed sum of between £20 and £400, in multiples of £5, every month for 12 months. You will then be issued with a yearly plan certificate. You must hold the certificate for a further four years to get the maximum return, at present approximately 5.85% p.a. over the five-year term. This is a good method of saving and the return is free of income tax and capital gains tax. Lower rates apply for early encashments.

NATIONAL SAVINGS INDEX-LINKED SAVINGS CERTIFICATES

The 8th Index-Linked Savings Certificates guarantee a return above the Retail Price Index (RPI) over a five-year term by offering extra tax-free interest in addition to indexation. The amount of extra interest added rises in each year as outlined below.

Tax-free return

year 1	RPI + 1.25% p.a., from date of purchase
year 2	RPI + 1.75% p.a., from date of purchase
year 3	RPI + 2.50% p.a., from date of purchase
year 4	RPI + 3.50% p.a., from date of purchase
year 5	RPI + 6.07% p.a., from date of purchase

The average interest rates work out at RPI plus 3% p.a. tax free.

You can earn both the index-linking and extra interest monthly from the date of purchase. This means that if you buy on the 15th, the value of your savings will change on the 15th of each following month. The maximum holding in 8th Index-Linked Issue Savings Certificates is £10,000. This is in addition to holdings of all other Issues of Savings Certificates.

As with National Savings Certificates, returns are exempt from income tax and capital gains tax.

Comment: Certificates are suitable for individuals who do not need immediate income but are seeking protection in real terms for their savings. Higher-rate taxpayers in this category will find the certificates particularly attractive.

INCOME BOND

Gross interest calculated at approximately 6.5% p.a. and is paid monthly. You may cash in part of your holding in multiples of £1,000 but you must keep a minimum balance of £2,000 in bonds (maximum £250,000).

The first payment is made on the next interest date after the bonds have been held for six weeks.

For repayments in the first year, interest is credited at half the rate from the date of purchase to the date of repayment on the amount repaid.

For repayments after the first year, interest is paid in full.

Normally, three months' notice of repayment is required.

Interest is taxable.

CAPITAL BONDS

National savings capital bonds offer a guaranteed rate of return over a five-year period. Interest rates rise each year so you must stay for the full five years to get the maximum return, average interest rates over 5 years are 7.75% p.a.

e.g. A £100 bond left on deposit for a five-year period commencing in November 1994 would yield as follow

	Total Repayable
After one year	£105.30
After two years	£111.51
After three years	£120.10
After four years	£130.91
After five years	£145.24

Comment :   *Interest is not paid out until the end of year five. However, interest earned is taxable annually.*

BANK DEPOSITS

Bank interest rates vary depending on which scheme you choose.

CURRENT ACCOUNTS

Many banks now pay interest on current accounts, provided you maintain a certain agreed minimum amount in the account. Withdrawals are by cheque, by cash machine or by calling into the Bank. Current Accounts are not really an efficient saving-mechanism, but more of a convenience.

DEMAND DEPOSIT ACCOUNTS

You keep an account of transactions in a Pass Book, interest is calculated daily and paid half-yearly and you can normally withdraw your money at any time.

Now, most banks also offer a Demand Deposit account which is operated through automatic tellers, giving you 24-hour access to withdraw or deposit money. However, you only begin to earn interest if a minimum amount is maintained in the account.

TIME DEPOSITS

As the name implies, these require that you leave a fixed amount of your money on deposit for a fixed period of time, so entitling you to a higher interest rate.

BUDGET ACCOUNTS

A budget account helps spread your household bills over a twelve-month period. You estimate your expected outlay for the next twelve months, and a monthly standing order is established from your current account for one-twelfth of this estimated figure. Your bills can be paid on receipt using overdraft facilities. Charges are usually the same as those for a current account plus an additional annual service charge.

Tax

Now, basic rate tax is deducted from deposit interest and people who are non tax-payers can reclaim this tax, or have the interest paid out gross, by completing form R85 at their local bank.

20% taxpayers can reclaim 5% of gross interest earned and higher-rate taxpayers are taxed on the gross interest at the difference between the basic rate and the higher rate (15%).

TESSAs

Anyone over eighteen who provides their name, address, date of birth and national insurance number can open a TESSA (Tax Exempt Special Savings Account) after the 1st January 1991.

TESSA's can earn interest tax-free, provided savings are left in the account for five years. Any interest withdrawn before the end of the five-year term is treated as taxable income for the year of withdrawal and the bank will deduct tax at the basic rate.

The most you can invest in a TESSA is £9,000 over five years. Up to £3,000 may be invested in the first year and up to £1,800 in each later year, provided you do not exceed £9,000 overall. Alternatively, you may save a regular amount, up to £150 a month.

If your savings are withdrawn before the end of the five-year term the account loses its tax-exemption status.

Higher-rate taxpayers

On the maturity of a TESSA, or on withdrawals of interest credited before the end of the five year period, higher-rate taxpayers do not have to pay any additional tax. However, if the TESSA is encashed early or loses its tax-exemption status, higher-rate taxpayers will have to pay tax at the difference between the basic rate 25% and 40%.

Bonuses and Penalties

If you move your money from one TESSA to another you will not lose any of the tax benefits, however, you may lose bonuses or suffer penalties. A typical bonus, payable at the end of a five year term, would be one or two per cent of the money invested in year one. Typical penalties would be thirty days interest or a fee of £25 on the transfer to a new TESSA.

Death during the term

If you die, all the capital and gross interest in the account is payable to your estate.

1994 Budget Changes

Tessas commenced on 1st January 1991 are due to mature on 1st January 1996. Holders of these mature accounts will be able to transfer the full amount of savings deposited in the first Tessa to a new Tessa Account. Interest already accumulated in the old Tessas cannot be transferred to new Tessas.

BUILDING SOCIETIES

DEPOSIT ACCOUNTS
Deposit accounts offer the lowest of building societies' interest rates, since, in the event of the society going under, depositors have first claim on the money that is left over.

SHARE ACCOUNTS
The most popular way for people to hold savings in building societies is by way of share accounts. They operate just like a deposit account and you can usually withdraw up to £1,000 on demand. To withdraw larger amounts, you may have to give advance notice and wait up to one month in some cases.

REGULAR SAVINGS ACCOUNTS
A straightforward way of rewarding the regular saver, these accounts require you to invest a specific amount on a monthly basis for an agreed length of time. In return, you get an interest rate normally 0.5% higher than the usual share account rate. A terminal bonus may also be paid after five years.

MONTHLY INCOME ACCOUNTS
If you need a regular income from your savings and you are prepared to make a minimum investment, which can be quite high, these accounts offer you monthly interest payments. Rates tend to be the same as those on share accounts but, in return for your agreement to certain restrictions on the amounts you may withdraw at any one time, some societies offer a higher rate.

TIME DEPOSITS
These require you to deposit a specific amount of money within set limits for an agreed length of time, usually one to five years. In return, you get a fixed-bonus rate over the share account rate which could be 0.5% to 2% higher. The obvious drawback to this kind of scheme is that the money is held under lock and key, to be had only at the end of the agreed term.

CURRENT ACCOUNTS
Building societies' facilities are now able to cope with your day-to-day finances. Many building societies have instant access accounts with a range of additional features which enable you to run your building society account as a direct replacement for a current bank account, with a cheque book, guarantee card, etc.

TAX

Basic rate tax is deducted from deposit interest and people who are non-taxpayers can claim back this tax or have the interest paid out gross by completing Form R85 at the local building society office.

A 20% tax payer can claim a 5% tax refund of gross interest earned and higher-rate taxpayers are taxed on the gross interest at the difference between the basic rate and the higher rate.

TESSAs

Anyone over eighteen who provides their name, address, date of birth and national insurance number can open a TESSA (Tax Exempt Special Savings Account) after the 1st January 1991.

TESSAs can earn interest tax-free, provided savings are left in the account for five years. Any interest withdrawn before the end of the five-year term is treated as taxable income for the year of withdrawal and the building society will deduct tax at the basic rate.

The most you can invest in a TESSA is £9,000 over five years. Up to £3,000 may be invested in the first year and up to £1,800 in each later year, provided you do not exceed the £9,000 overall maximum. Alternatively, you may save a regular amount, up to £150 a month.

Savings may not be withdrawn until the end of the five-year term without the account losing its tax-exemption status.

Higher-rate taxpayers

On the maturity of a TESSA, or on withdrawals of interest credited, higher-rate taxpayers do not pay additional tax. However, if the TESSA is encashed early or loses its tax-exemption status, higher-rate taxpayers do pay additional tax.

Bonuses and Penalties

If you move your money from one TESSA to another you will not lose any of the tax benefits, however, you may lose bonuses or suffer penalties. A typical bonus, payable at the end of a five year term, would be one or two per cent of the money invested in year one. Typical penalties would be thirty days interest or a fee of £25 on the transfer to a new TESSA Account.

Death during the term

If you die, all the capital and gross interest in the account is payable to your estate. Further information is available on Inland Revenue leaflet IR114.

1994 Budget Changes

Tessas commenced on 1st January 1991 are due to mature on 1st January 1996. Holders of these mature accounts will be able to transfer the full amount of savings deposited in the first Tessa to a new Tessa Account. Interest already accumulated in the old Tessas cannot be transferred to new Tessas.

Offshore Accounts

Interest rates offered on cash deposit are now generally low, so you may like to search out new ways of maximising your returns. On this front, one little used avenue is offshore building society accounts.

The advantages of using off shore building society accounts are:

- the gross rate of interest paid is normally higher in offshore accounts as opposed to that paid in onshore accounts.
- your interest is paid gross and while your tax liability cannot be avoided it may be delayed.

NOTE: The UK's Building Society Deposit Protection Scheme does not cover offshore accounts. However, Section 22 of the Building Societies Act requires all the liabilities of a subsidiary company to be guaranteed by the parent company.

REGULAR SAVINGS WITH LIFE ASSURANCE

The two main types of plan under which you save with Life Assurance Companies are:
- Traditional Endowment Plans
- Unit-Linked Endowment Plans

ENDOWMENTS
Without-Profits Plan

With Endowment Assurance, you save in agreed instalments over a period of time, at the end of which a guaranteed sum is paid. This is known as a without-profits endowment plan.

With-Profits Plans

Under these plans, the company invests your premiums across a wide selection of assets such as Property, Shares, Government Stocks and so on. If these investments yield more than the amount that has already been guaranteed, and they usually do, bonuses are declared and the bonuses are added to the guaranteed sum you receive.

Bonuses can be Reversionary, which means that they are added to your guaranteed amount once a year; or they can be Terminal, which means that a once-off bonus is paid to you when the policy has completed its agreed term or on your death. Terminal bonuses can be substantial, but they are not guaranteed.

Comment: To date, Endowment Assurance Plans have generally yielded very good returns and are a relatively stable investment in recessionary times.

                However, you may have to wait until the end of the agreed term to benefit from the Terminal Bonus and so get the maximum possible return on your investment.

Unit-Linked Plans

Basically, Unit-Linked Plans enable you to become involved in different investments side by side with the "big guys". The monies paid in by a number of individuals are banded together into a portfolio of investments which are managed on a day to day basis by investment experts.

There is no limit on the amounts you can pay into unit linked plans. The money you pay goes to buy units in the portfolio of investments - the number of units you receive depends on the amount you choose to invest. The value of the units which you hold is increased by the profits earned on the portfolio of investments, after management expenses and tax have been paid.

LIFE ASSURANCE AND UNIT-LINKED PLANS

These combine straightforward investment with Life Assurance cover. You agree to pay premiums on a regular basis, over a number of years. Each premium then has a percentage deducted from it - how much depends on your age, occupation and your general state of health. This deduction is then used to purchase your Life Assurance cover and to pay for the company's management expenses. The balance of each premium purchases units in the life assurance company's investment portfolio, at whatever the Unit Price is at that time.

If you discontinue your premiums at any stage, your life assurance policy is either surrendered or made fully paid-up. It is worth keeping in mind that the surrender-value of Unit-Linked policies may only be attractive after approximately ten or more years.

TAX AND LIFE ASSURANCE
Qualifying and non-qualifying policies.

The tax treatment of life assurance policies depends to a large extent on whether the policy is a qualifying or non-qualifying policy. A qualifying policy must be certified as such by the Inland Revenue. Generally, it is one where the premium is paid regularly, at least once a year over a period of ten or more years, and has a minimum guaranteed-sum assured payable at death.

The proceeds from a qualifying policy are generally tax-free, assuming it was in force for the required minimum term.

Also, remember that if a qualifying policy was issued before the 14th March 1984 on your own life or that of your spouse, you may be entitled to claim some tax relief on the premiums paid.

Non-Qualifying Policy

Up to 5% of the premium or premiums paid may be withdrawn annually tax-free, other gains from a non-qualifying policy may be subject to some tax on death, maturity, sale or encashment. Normally, the taxable gain on a non-qualifying policy is its excess cash value on termination or encashment, after account has been taken of previous withdrawals and the premium or premiums paid.

This taxable gain is added to your income -

If you were a higher-rate taxpayer before this gain is added to your income, you pay additional tax on the gain at 15%, i.e. the difference between basic-rate and higher-rate tax.

If you are a basic-rate taxpayer after this gain is added to your income, you pay no additional tax.

If you were a basic-rate taxpayer before this gain is added to your income, but a higher-rate taxpayer after the gain is added to your income, you may claim top slicing relief, see page 169 for details.

SHARES

The primary purpose of the stock exchange is to help companies raise capital to finance industrial commercial expansion. So, when you buy shares in a company you become a part-owner of that company. Being a part-owner entitles you to a small percentage of the profits, by way of dividend normally paid twice annually.

Unlike the income from a bank or building society, dividends are not directly related to the money invested but are linked to growth in the company's future profits and dividend policy. However, when you buy shares you may be more interested in the capital growth of your investment i.e. the increase in stock exchange value of your shares.

When you buy shares there is always the risk of a bad investment and that you may lose some or all of your money. This risk may diminish over time, provided you choose well and spread your risks. This is why shares are so popular with insurance companies and pension funds as an investment medium.

However, if you are going to need your money next month or next year, shares are not for you and you would be much better-off putting your money in a more secure place. On the other hand, if you can wait for five, ten, or twenty years for your investment to mature and you can cope with the "crashes" along the way, then shares are likely to give you a very good return.

SHARE PERFORMANCE

If you decide to invest in shares you may wish to keep in touch with their progress by reading the financial pages of your daily newspaper. At first sight, these financial pages can be very puzzling. However, they will keep you up to date and contain much useful information.

A typical section of a financial paper would look like this:

High	Low	Company	Price	+ / -	Div. Net	C'vr	D/Y G'rs.	P/E
440	346	Legal & General	358xd	+ 3	15.8	1.0	5.9	23.7
350	261	Sun Alliance Grp	271xd	+ 1	12.5	2.0	6.2	9.9
321	267	Lloyd Thompson 5p	268	- 1	7.5	φ	3.8	φ
1	2	3	4	5	6	7	8	9

Highs and Lows

The first column usually gives the highest price paid for that individual share in the current year and the second column gives the lowest price. The idea is to buy as close as possible to the lowest price and sell as close as possible to the highest.

Company

Column three gives the stock or share name and sometimes its nominal value. The nominal value is of no real interest to the investor. It is the price the shares were originally issued at.

Price

Column four gives the share price which is usually the last official price paid on the market for the shares.

Ex-Dividend

As we said earlier, companies usually pay dividends twice a year. About six to eight weeks before a dividend is paid, the directors announce what the next dividend will be. A week or two after this announcement, the company's share register is temporarily closed. The coming dividend is paid only to those people who are on the register of shareholders on that day and the company's shares then go ex-dividend and are marked xd in your paper. So, if you buy shares marked xd you will not get the upcoming dividend.

Rise or Fall

Column five gives the difference between opening and closing prices of each share in the previous day's trading.

Dividend Net

Column six gives the net dividend payable. So, if you had 100 shares in Legal & General you would get a dividend warrant or cheque for £15.80. Tax at 20% will already have been deducted and this tax may be reclaimed if you are a non-taxpayer.

Cover (C'vr)

Column seven gives the dividend cover which is the ratio of the last year's profits to the dividends paid: in Legal & General's case this is 1. In other words, if Legal & General had paid out all its profits to shareholders, the dividend would have been twice that actually paid. Approximately 50% of Legal & General's profits were retained by the directors to help generate future profits.

Dividend Yield (D/Y)

The dividend yield is the ratio of the annual dividend from a share to its share price. Column eight normally gives the dividend yield gross i.e.before tax.

Price-Earnings Ratio (PE)

Column nine gives the price-earnings ratio. Traditionally, many people related a share price to a company's net assets. Another way of valuing a share is to relate the share price to a company's flow of profits and this is known as its price-earnings ratio.

Price-earnings ratio is calculated by dividing the company's share price by after-tax earnings due to that share over its most recent financial year. The ratio is sometimes calculated using expected rather than historical earnings. A high price-earnings ratio shows that investors have a lot of confidence in the company's future prosperity. A low P/E ratio can mean that the investor is getting earnings "cheap" or may imply lack of confidence in that company's future prosperity.

Tax

For basic rate taxpayers dividends are subject to income tax at 20% only and this tax is normally deducted at source.

If you are a non-taxpayer, you may reclaim this tax and if you are a higher-rate taxpayer you pay additional tax at the difference between tax at 20% and tax at 40%.

You may also be liable to pay capital gains tax at your appropriate income-tax rate on any profit you make when selling your shares, unless your taxable gain falls within your capital gains tax exemption limit - £5,800 in the 1994/95 and £6,000 1995/96 tax year.

PERSONAL EQUITY PLAN

Obviously, if you invest in shares without paying tax on dividend income and capital growth earned, your returns would, on average, be much higher. Personal Equity Plans (PEPs) allow you to invest in shares, unit and investment trusts without incurring either income or capital gains tax, provided your investments are within defined limits. To invest in a PEP, you must be over eighteen years of age and resident in the UK for tax purposes.

PEPs were first introduced in 1987 to encourage direct investment in UK companies. However, because of the many restrictions imposed they were not as effective as was first thought. The 1989 Finance Act removed many of these restrictions.

Investing in a PEP

You can now invest up to £6,000 a year in a personal equity plan. This can include up to £6,000 in unit trusts or investment trust company shares from 6th April 1992, provided at least 50% of the trust's investment is in EC member states company shares. You can invest through a "plan manager" which may be your bank, building society or other investment adviser. The plan manager deals with all the administration - buying and selling the shares and collecting dividends etc. Normally, you cannot transfer shares you already own into a PEP scheme. However, new issues or privatisation may be included, provided your plan manager agrees. You can also accumulate cash in a PEP, so you do not have to invest in shares straight away.

In the 1994 Budget the Chancellor extended the range of eligible investments to include certain fixed interest securities, corporate bonds and convertible preference shares in EC companies from 6th April 1995.

Single Company PEP

From the 1st January 1992, it is also possible to invest up to £3,000 in a single company PEP, in addition to £6,000 in a general PEP.

Discretionary PEPs

In a discretionary PEP, your money is pooled with that of other investors and the plan manager chooses investments into which your money goes.

Non-Discretionary PEPs

You choose the investment and your plan manager buys and sells shares on your instructions. The advantage of this method is that you can plan your buying and selling over a period of time and thus build up a portfolio with a spread of shares, thereby reducing your long-term risks.

Tax

Dividends are free of income tax. This applies whether the income is paid to you directly, or reinvested in the PEP - it is the job of the plan manager to reclaim any tax paid on dividends at source etc. One of the major attractions of PEPs is that any capital gain arising from a disposal of shares does not incur any liability to capital gains tax. Basic-rate tax is deducted from any interest you receive on cash invested in a PEP and higher-rate taxpayers pay extra tax at the end of the tax year.

Comment:　　A well-chosen Personal Equity Plan with low charges is a good long-term investment for most taxpayers.

UNIT TRUSTS

Unit trusts can be a way of investing in company shares, they can be more convenient and less risky than investing directly in the stock market. Over the last fifteen years, the returns from Unit Trusts compare very favourably with other traditional investment mechanisms.

INVESTING IN UNIT TRUSTS

When you invest in unit trusts, you buy units from the trust management company. When you cash in your investment, you sell units back to the management company. The management company uses the cash you pay for units to buy investments.

INCOME OR CAPITAL

Your return from unit trusts comes in two ways:

Income: Dividends from shares the Unit Trust buys.

Capital Growth: The increase in the price of shares the Unit Trust buys.

Some unit trusts specialise in buying company shares which pay higher than average dividends and so can distribute higher than average income. This type of trust is known as an "income trust" and is suitable if you require a regular income from your investment.

If you do not want a regular income from your investment, but simply want to see your investment grow, you should invest in a "growth trust". A growth trust invests your money in companies whose share price is expected to rise substantially but whose dividend payments may well be low.

TAXATION

Investment in unit trusts can give rise to income tax and capital gains tax, unless you invest through a Personal Equity Plan. The income you receive from a unit trust is paid net of tax at 20%. For basic rate tax payers this 20% deduction will satisfy their tax liability. Higher-rate taxpayers pay additional tax on this income at the difference between 20% and the higher rate of 40%.

Capital gains tax is payable at your relevant income-tax rate on any taxable capital gain. Your taxable gain for the purposes of capital gains tax is the gain on your investment, less indexation relief and your appropriate annual allowance up to £5,800 in 1994/95 and £6,000 in the 1995/96 tax year.

INVESTMENT TRUSTS

In an investment trust, you purchase shares in the trust company, which in turn invests the majority of its resources in the stocks and shares of other companies. So, you share in the capital and income of the investment trust's portfolio of investments.

In many cases, the shares of the investment trust are priced at a discount i.e. below their net asset value. This may provide you with a higher level of income and capital growth than you might expect by investing directly in the stock market or through unit trusts.

TAX

Income tax at 20% is deducted at source from dividends. This may be reclaimed by non-taxpayers, while higher-rate taxpayers suffer additional tax. On the sale of shares, capital gains tax may also be payable within the normal indexation and annual exemption rules.

OFFSHORE FUNDS

Offshore funds are normally located in a tax haven and are structured as unit trusts or investment trusts, specialising in equities, foreign currencies and foreign government stocks.

Depending on their tax status under UK law, offshore funds may be classified as Distributor Funds or Accumulator Funds.

A fund will normally be classified as a distributor fund if it distributes 85% of the income which would have been liable to corporation tax had the fund been operating in the UK

Accumulator Funds

Here, little or no dividends are paid and the gross income is accumulated within the fund until you dispose of your investment. On disposal, tax charges may arise on the capital gain and on the "income rolled-up".

This may be tax-efficient planning if you intend being a non-taxpayer or a lower-rate taxpayer by the time you decide to cash in your offshore investment.

UK-Resident

Dividends are normally paid gross and are taxable under Schedule D Case VI on a prior-year basis.

Capital gains tax will be payable in the normal manner on gains arising on disposal.

If you are resident but not domiciled in the UK, you will be subject to UK tax on income and capital gains only to the extent that they are remitted to the UK.

Overseas-Investors

There is no liability to UK tax, and overseas investors will be taxed in accordance with the laws of the country in which they are resident.

ENTERPRISE INVESTMENT SCHEMES (EIS)

EIS was introduced in 1993 to provide expertise and new equity investment in unquoted trading companies.

Income tax relief is available on investments in qualifying companies up to £100,000 annually. To qualify a company must carry on a qualifying activity for a minimum period of five years. There is a limit of £1m on the maximum amount a company can raise under this scheme in any one year, however a higher limit of £5m applies to companies engaged in certain shipping activities.

To qualify for EIS investment a company's business activities must not consist to any substantial extent of any of the following:

- dealing in land, in commodities or futures or in shares, securities or other financial instruments.

- dealing in goods otherwise than in the course of any ordinary trade of wholesale or retail distribution.

- banking, insurance, money-lending, debt-factoring, hire-purchase, financial or other financial activities.

- oil extraction activities.

- leasing (including letting ships or charter or other assets on hire) or receiving royalties or licence fees.

- providing legal or accountancy services.

TAX

Income tax relief at 20% is available in the tax year you subscribe for EIS shares. This relief is clawed back if you dispose of the shares within five years unless the disposal occurs on the company's liquidation. If the company goes into liquidation and you suffer financial loss within the first five years, further income tax or capital gains tax relief may be claimed.

Example:

You invest £50,000 under the 'EIS company. You receive £10,000 of a tax refund i.e. 20% of £50,000. If your entire investment is written off on the liquidation of the company after two years, so, you suffer a Capital loss of £40,000 (£50,000 less £10,000).

You will be entitled to offset this capital loss against your taxable income or have it relieved against a capital gain in that relevant tax year.

DISPOSAL AFTER FIVE YEARS

Once the shares have been held for five years, there is no income tax claw back or capital gains tax penalties when the shares are sold. However if you suffer a capital nett loss on the disposal of the shares you can have this loss offset against taxable income or have it relieved against a capital gain in the relevant tax year.

1994 BUDGET CHANGES

In the 1994 Budget the Chancellor added capital gain tax "roll over" to EIS investment for gains realised after 29th November 1994. This roll over relief can be claimed provided the proceeds from the gain are reinvested in an EIS company.

VENTURE CAPITAL TRUSTS

Venture Capital Trusts (VCT) are pooled EIS funds established by city institutions for investments in a range of qualifying EIS companies.

From 6th April 1995 you can invest in Venture Capital Trusts with 20% income tax relief and also with capital gains tax roll over relief if applicable. VCTs investors can also avail of the other tax benefit available under single EIS investments.

BRITISH GOVERNMENT STOCKS

British Government stocks are Government borrowings from the public, usually at a guaranteed rate of interest.

Stocks have a nominal or face-value, usually in units of £100. So, for each £100 of nominal stock you hold, you are guaranteed to get a £100 cash from the Government for it at some time in the future.

Coupon

Coupon is a term used on the stock exchange to describe the rate of interest paid on a fixed-interest stock. It tells you the gross interest before tax which the stock pays out and is expressed as a percentage of the nominal value. e.g. 9% Treasury Loan 1994.

Redemption Date

Following the name and the coupon, is a year. This is the date on which the Government has promised to redeem the stock.

The date may be a range of years, for example 9% Treasury Loan 1992/96. In this case, the Government can choose in which year out of this range of years to redeem the stock.

With a few stocks, the coupon is followed by a year and the words *or after,* for example: 3.5% War Loan 1952 or after. This means that the Government may redeem the stock in 1952 or in any later year it decides. Stocks which have no definite year quoted are called *undated stocks.*

Stocks Classification

Stocks are generally classified under four groups, according to the length of time left until redemption.

- Short-dated stocks: stocks are redeemable in the next five years.

- Medium-dated stocks: the latest redemption date is more than five years but less than fifteen years.

- Long-dated stocks: the latest redemption date is over fifteen years.

- Undated stocks: no definite redemption date is applicable.

Price changes

The stock exchange is a rather nervous place and the value of your stock may be affected by many factors e.g. a political crisis or a bad economic forecast. However, the most relevant factors are usually interest rates and your stock redemption-date.

The cash value of your stock will normally fluctuate with changes in interest rates. So, if interest rates go up, the value of your stock will fall and vice versa. However, the size of this fluctuation is also determined by the redemption date.

Example:

Interest rates are 10% and you have a £100 in undated stock. If interest rates go up to 15%, the market value of your stock will have to fall by approximately one third to give you the equivalent of 15% return on your investment.

However, if your stock redemption-date was only a year off, the market value of your stock would not need to fall by a third to give a 15% return on your investment over a year when the cash discount value of your stock is taken into account.

INDEX-LINKED GILTS

Index-linked gilts are similar to fixed-interest gilts, the main difference being that the interest payments and the value at redemption are linked to the retail price index (RPI). Index-linked gilts offer a secure shelter for capital in times of inflation and may provide a higher rate of return than conventional gilts.

Tax

British Government stocks are free of capital gains tax. However, you pay income tax on the interest you get from stocks at your relevant rate of tax.

If you buy stocks through the National Savings Stock Register, interest is paid gross. If you buy through a stockbroker, interest is normally paid net of tax.

Interest payments are made on Government gilts twice a year. You are entitled to receive the interest payments if you hold the security on a specified date. If a stock is sold after this date, it is said to be sold "ex div"; a stock sold before this date is sold "cum div".

Cum-dividend and ex-dividend

If you buy or sell gilts before the specified date the purchase price will take into account accrued interest. This accrued interest is subject to income tax unless the total nominal value of all the stocks you hold is £5,000 or less.

Your contract note shows the amount of accrued interest involved in each transaction. Accrued interest is taxed as follows:

- If you sell cum-dividend, you are taxed on the accrued interest included in the price you receive.
- If you sell ex-dividend, you get tax relief on the accrued interest that has been deducted from the quoted price.
- If you buy cum-dividend, you get tax relief on the accrued interest included in the price you pay.
- If you buy ex-dividend, you are taxed on the accrued interest which has been deducted from the price paid.

For more details about the way accrued interest is taxed, see Inland Revenue leaflet IR 68.

BORROWING

Borrowing is the area where many people come unstuck - even those who otherwise plan their finances soundly and prudently. Before planning to raise any loan, there are a number of points you should keep firmly in mind.

Duration of Borrowing

Borrowing normally can be classified under two headings:

- short term borrowing i.e. borrowings for less than ten years
- long term borrowing i.e. borrowings for more than ten years.

Risks

A major risk in borrowing is that of a serious change in your personal circumstances. For instance, what would happen in the event of sickness, death, redundancy, or any other development which might reduce your ability to repay the loan? Also, look at the other side, should you wish to repay the loan early would there be any penalties?

Rate of Interest Charged

Because of the 1984 Consumer Credit Act, all lenders must now quote you their Annual Percentage Rate (APR) on interest and other charges before you take out a loan. However, should you wish to calculate the real annual rate yourself, you may do so with the following formula:

$$\frac{200 \times A \times B}{D(C+1) + B/3(C-3A+2)}$$

A = number of instalments each year.
B = total interest charged
C = total number of instalments
D = amount borrowed

Taxation

A guiding principle of any borrowing should be that the money will be raised in such a way as to receive the maximum tax relief. Some avenues are more tax-efficient than others.

BORROWING

Most people borrowing money do so from one of the following sources:

Banks	Hire-Purchase Companies
Building Societies	Credit Cards

Now, we will have a look at what each offer you when you go shopping for money.

BANKS

There are three principal ways of borrowing money from banks.

Overdrafts

Overdrafts or cheque book accounts are normally the simplest type of bank loan for short-term borrowing. Basically, you agree the loan amount with your bank manager and then draw on it using your cheque book or cash card. The advantage of this system is that you only pay interest on the actual amount you need on a day-to-day basis. By crossing a cheque i.e. drawing two parallel lines across it, you give yourself greater protection in the event of it being lost; as the crossing ensures that the cheque must be lodged in a bank account. Most major banks now offer current accounts that pay interest on your bank balance and free-banking, if you stay in credit. However, if you go overdrawn from time to time the charges can be steep. A general guide to bank charges at December 1994 is outlined on page 29. Many banks make their charges on a monthly or quarterly basis; however, for the purpose of this illustration all charges are calculated to give the approximate costs on an annual basis on borrowings of £500.

Budget Accounts

Budget accounts are like current accounts with a built-in overdraft. They are intended to help you meet irregular bills by saving regularly. You pay a monthly instalment based on the total of your expected annual household expenditure. If there is not enough money in your account to cover a bill, the overdraft facility comes into play. However, they can be relatively expensive: the interest rate tends to be high and not all accounts pay you interest while you are in credit.

Term Loans

As the name implies, these are loans for an agreed amount of money with the repayments spread over an agreed amount of time. Unlike an overdraft, the agreed amount of money is given to you in one lump sum and the interest on the total is charged from the outset. Normally, repayments are made monthly over the agreed life of the loan.

A Guide to
BANKING CHARGES

Bank	Account	Annual Fees if Overdrawn	Annual Interest Charges		O/D Letter	Bounced Cheque	Stop Cheque
			Authorised Borrowings	Unauthorised Borrowings			
Abbey National	Current	None	9.9%	29.5%	£5.00	£20.00	None
Bank of Scotland	Chequeplus	£102	12.0%	20.0%	£15.00	£20.00	£10.00
Barclays	Interest	£180	19.2%	29.8%	None	£25.00	£8.00
Clydesdale Bank	Flexicash	£160	22.7%	33.5%	£10.00	£25.00	£6.00
Co-Op	Current	£120	18.0%	28.8%	None	£30.00	£8.00
Girobank	Keyway	£180	11.8%	26.4%	None	£25.00	£10.00
Lloyds	Classic	£96	19.4%	26.8%	£7.00	£25.00	£8.00
Midland	Orchard	£204	16.7%	26.0%	None	£25.00	£6.00
Natwest	Current Plus	£108	17.5%	29.5%	None	£27.50	£7.00
Royal Bank of Scotland	Current	£120	18.1%	27.0%	£15.00	£25.00	£10.00
TSB	Interest Plus	£72	18.8%	29.8%	None	£17.50	None
Yorkshire	Paymaster Plus	£108	19.3%	30.6%	£15.00	£20.00	None

December 1994

O/D = Over drawn

Home Improvement Loans

Home improvement loans usually have a lower rate of interest and a longer repayment term than other types of loans. However, you may be required to provide extra security for a home improvement loan.

Bridging Loans

Bridging loans are short-term loans, used to finance buying a new home or selling your old home. A 'closed' bridging loan is used if you have bought your new home and have exchanged contracts on the sale of your old home. An 'open' bridging loan is required where you have exchanged contracts on your new home but not on your old home.

Mortgages

Nowadays, the main banks also offer home mortgages. The interest rates may be higher than those of building societies but they have become much more competitive in recent years.

HIRE-PURCHASE COMPANIES

A bit of a minefield! Hire-purchase is normally very expensive because of the high interest rates charged, the high administration costs and the fact that you have to pay VAT on the hire-purchase charges. Often, too, there are substantial penalties involved in settling the loan at an earlier date than that agreed at the outset.

For instance, if you buy a car on hire-purchase over a three-year period and you decide to change your car before the end of the term, your settlement figure with the hire-purchase company may be the total monthly repayments outstanding, rather than the outstanding loan balance at that date.

BUILDING SOCIETIES

Traditionally, loans were available from building societies only for the purchase of a new home or for the improvement of your existing home.

The amount which may be borrowed for these purposes depends on:

- your income! You can borrow up to three-times the main breadwinner's annual income, plus one and maybe one-and-a-half-times your partner's income. However, some lenders give up to two-and-a-half-times joint incomes.
- the value of the property, or the cost of the improvement, as decreed by the building society's own surveyor.

Building societies lend money using the home you buy as their security. They hold the deeds of your home until the mortgage is repaid in full. If the loan you require is above their normal thresholds, they may also require a mortgage indemnity policy.

Mortgage Indemnity Policy

Many building societies are prepared to lend more money if you are able to provide extra security. One way of doing this is through a mortgage indemnity policy. This insurance policy guarantees the society repayment of your loan in full in the event of a repossession or in the event of the sale of your home for less than the outstanding mortgage balance.

House Insurance

Normally, you would be required to insure your home in order to protect the building society's interest in the property, so, that, in the event of its destruction, funds are available for the mortgage to be repaid or the home to be rebuilt.

A Mortgage Protection Policy

The society may require you to take out a mortgage protection policy (a relative of Life Assurance) to provide for the repayment of the mortgage in full, in the event of your death or that of your partner.

Current Accounts

Many building societies have introduced bank-like current accounts offering:
- cheque books
- cash dispenser withdrawals
- salary in-payments
- bill-paying services
- overdraft facilities

The charges for current accounts with building societies will normally work out at less than the corresponding charges with banks. However, all building societies reserve the right to make additional charges which will normally only be levied on customers who persist in spending beyond their authorised limit. You can pay interest on your overdrawn account at anything from around 10% APR up to almost 35% APR, depending on the size of your facility and on whether your overdraft has been formally authorised or not. Building societies normally pay you interest on your account while it is in credit.

CREDIT CARDS

Credit cards have now become a widely accepted mode of payment. The name credit card covers a very broad area and can include bank credit cards such as Access and Visa, chargecards like American Express and Diners Club, Gold and Platinum cards for high spenders and finally retail store cards.
Access and Visa cards are available within a wide range of banks, building societies and other financial establishments all over Britain. On an individual basis, there is little difference between the major cards. However, when it comes to the actual financial establishment operating these cards there may be wide variations between the annual charges paid and interest rates applicable to outstanding balances.

So, your first step towards avoiding excessive charges on your credit card is to understand how it works and make sure you get an estimate of what your annual charges are likely to be.

Bank Credit Cards

With a bank credit card you are billed for your purchase once a month and then you usually have 21 days to pay the full amount or to make the minimum repayment using your card's built-in credit facility. If the full amount is paid before the due date, no interest is charged. However, if the amount in full is not paid by the due date, interest at approximately 28% p.a. is payable from the date of the statement or from the date of transaction. Interest is normally charged on cash withdrawals from the date of the withdrawal.

A feature offered by many credit card companies is Credit Protection. This insurance plan protects you if you become unable to repay your credit card balance due to sickness, death or redundancy. It costs approximately 60p for every £100 outstanding. Be careful if you do not wish to avail of this benefit as many credit card companies will enrol you for it automaticallly.

Gold Cards

You will need to earn at least £20,000 p.a. to get a Gold Card. The perks you will get vary from card to card but will probably include an unsecured overdraft at a reasonable rate, increased cash withdrawal facilities at banks or cash dispenser machines and a range of insurance benefits.

However, subscriptions are not cheap, you could pay up to £90 annually for the privilege of having a gold card and a further £30 p.a. for your partner.

So, before you go for gold, look at the perks which you could actually use. An automatic overdraft of £10,000 at a reduced rate can be among the cheapest ways of borrowing, even after taking into account your subscriptions and enrolment fees.

Insurance is another way in which gold cards can save you money. Many gold cards offer 90 days purchase protection insurance, so that if you buy goods with your gold card which are stolen, lost or damaged within 90 days of purchase, you can claim a refund. Holiday Insurance is also available free if you pay for the holiday with your gold card and this can include - injury compensation insurance up to £250,000, flight delay compensation of around £200 and lost luggage compensation up to £1,000.

Store Cards

A large proportion of retail store cards operate as "option accounts" and they work in a similar way to bank credit cards. You have the choice of settling outstanding amounts in full at the end of the interest-free period or you make the minimum repayment using the in-built credit facility. Interest is payable on the outstanding balance at approximately 30% p.a.

Approximately one third of retail store cards operate as "Budget Accounts". Here, you agree to pay a monthly sum to the retail store and in return it will give you a credit limit for purchases somewhere between 18 and 30 times this montly repayment. Interest is normally charged on outstanding balance.

Budget accounts can suit younger shoppers or people with tight budgets as they may find them preferable to use and easier to obtain than credit cards. They also impose more self-dicipline on your spending, than credit cards do.

BUYING A HOME

This is probably the largest single expenditure in the life of many people, and sadly, one that is made while many have relatively little experience of financial matters. So, before you commit yourself to a property make absolutely sure you understand the full implications of what you are undertaking. Home ownership brings with it many hidden costs and responsibilities that may not at first be readily apparent.

Here we outline a home buying plan under three headings:

THE DEPOSIT
HIDDEN COSTS
MORTGAGE

THE DEPOSIT

Definitely, a building society is a good place to start accumulating the deposit for a home, as they look more favourably on savers when the time comes around to apply for a mortgage.

A point to bear in mind when puzzling over which building society to choose, is the size of the mortgage you will eventually be likely to be looking for and whether a particular society or bank will grant you an 80%, 90% or a 100% mortgage.

A tax-efficient saving plan for a home deposit could be commenced as soon as you get your first pay-packet, by allocating a small sum each month to one of the saving schemes outlined earlier in this guide.

HIDDEN COSTS
For the house-purchaser, there are many hidden costs within the broader context of home purchase. Here is a brief check list which you may find useful.

Solicitor's Conveyancer's fee - Your Own	
Solicitor's Fees - The Lender's	
Surveyor's fee	
Land registry fee	
Stamp Duty	

Valuer's Fees - Your Own	
Valuer's Fees - The Lender's	
Fees for specialist tests	
Mortgage indemnity policy	
Fire Insurance	

House-hunting expenses	
Removal expenses	
Cost of disconnection & reconnection of services	
Basic Furniture & Fittings	
Carpets etc.	

MORTGAGE

In these days of easy credit, obtaining a mortage is not difficult. In fact, many lenders now provide mortgage certificates to home hunters to enable them to buy the home of their choice, with the assurance of a mortgage approval 'in their pocket'.

One of the key incentives to home purchase is the tax relief on mortgage interest paid. The first £30,000 of your mortgage qualifies for tax relief at the 15% rate in the 1995/96 tax year. The tax relief on mortgage interest is normally claimed through MIRAS (Mortgage Interest Relief At Source). This means that interest payments on many mortgages are paid net of the 25% rate in the 1995/96 tax year.

MORTGAGE REPAYMENT METHODS

Although the nominal term of a mortgage is usually 25 years, in practice, many mortgages last for less then ten years. Even so, when deciding which type of mortgage is best for you, you should take into consideration your long-term needs, as well as your short-term commitments. Here, we summarise the main types of mortgage and the repayment methods currently available.

Annuity Mortgage

Under an annuity mortgage, your monthly repayments consist of both capital and interest. In the early years, interest represents the larger part of each monthly repayment. Then, as more and more capital is repaid, the balance changes and towards the end of your mortgage term, the vast majority of your monthly repayment is paying off your loan balance.

One of the main attractions of an annuity-type mortgage is that it may be less costly in the early years, at a time when most home buyers are feeling the greatest cash drain. Traditionally it has not been the most cost effective long term. However, this may now very well have changed with the virtual elimination of mortgage interest relief.

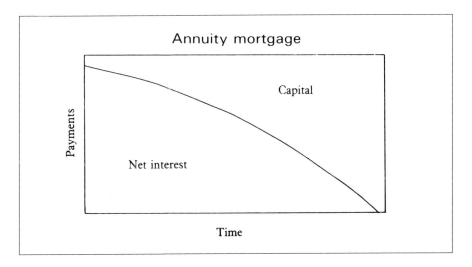

Mortgage Protection Policy

Normally, under an annuity plan, the lender will require that you take out a mortgage protection policy to repay the mortgage in the event of you or your spouse's premature death.

Interest-Only Mortgage

Under an interest-only mortgage, you take out an interest-only loan for, say, 25 years. At the same time, you commence an investment plan which will also mature in 25 years time. Tax relief will continue to be available on the interest payments, within the normal limits. Towards the end of the mortgage period, you normally find that your investment plan's encashment value may exceed the initial projections, so you can either repay your mortgage early or go on to create a cash bonus for yourself at the end of the normal term. There are many ways of creating a fund to pay off your mortgage at the end of the mortgage term - some are detailed below.

With-Profits Endowment Assurance

Under these plans you pay a level premium into a life assurance endowment plan. Your premiums are invested across a wide selection of assets, such as property, shares or government stocks. If these investments yield more than the amount that has already been guaranteed, and they usually do, bonuses are declared and the bonuses are added to the guaranteed-sum you receive.

Bonuses can be Reversionary, which means they are added to the guaranteed amount once a year, or they can be Terminal, which means a once-off bonus is paid to you when the policy has completed its agreed term.

Low-start Endowment Mortgage

Here, monthly premiums start at a lower level than for a conventional endowment plan, usually levelling off after the first five or ten years. Many low-start schemes are geared specifically for borrowers whose income is expected to rise at a sufficient rate to meet these rising premium-costs.

Unit-Linked Mortgages

Unit-Linked Plans are normally considerably more speculative than the traditional with-profits endowment plans. The money you pay goes to buy units in a portfolio of investments; the number of units you receive depends on the value of the units at the time you buy and the amount of money invested. The value of your units is increased by the profits earned on the portfolio of investments, after a fixed amount has been deducted for management expenses and tax.

Unit-linked mortgages are a relatively recent development. One problem normally associated with them is that their day-to-day value may depend to a relatively large extent on the performance of the stock market.

This means that if the underlying investments perform well, the rewards could be greater than under a with-profits endowment plan. If, on the other hand, they do badly, you may be called upon to increase your premiums later to make up the shortfall.

Pension-Linked Mortgage

The benefits from a pension plan are normally paid in two ways:

- A lifetime pension or annuity at retirement.
- A tax-free lump sum and a smaller pension or annuity at retirement.

It is this tax-free lump sum benefit that provides the basis for a pension-linked mortgage.

The workings of a pension-linked mortgage are similar to the workings of an endowment mortgage. You pay interest-only over the mortgage term and when you come to retirement age, you take part of your pension fund as a tax-free cash lump sum to repay the mortgage.

The advantages of a pension-linked mortgage over an endowment mortgage are based on tax relief. Not only do you get tax relief on the mortgage interest payments, but you also get tax relief on the contributions you make to the pension plan. Pension plans also grow at a higher rate than normal investment as they have less tax to pay.

Because you can only take part of your pension fund in cash, pension-linked mortgages may initially require a greater monthly outlay than a comparable annuity or endowment mortgage. However, the ultimate benefits may be significantly greater.

Another important point to bear in mind when you are considering a pension-linked mortgage is the fact that you are repaying your mortgage out of retirement income, which may have its own consequences in the long term.

Unit Trusts or PEP Mortgages

Unit Trusts and PEP mortgages are relatively new and are probably more suitable to the borrower who is more financially aware. The method of repayment is similar to an endowment mortgage, as you agree to make a regular payment into a Unit Trust plan or a PEP (personal equity plan) over the term of the mortgage. The main advantage of Unit Trust and PEPs lies in their more favourable tax treatment, together with their potential for better performance over a long number of years.

Foreign Currency Loans.

A number of lenders now make loans available in currencies other than Sterling. At times when UK interest rates had been substantially higher than interest rates in other currencies, such loans were an attractive means of reducing repayments. The inherent currency risks involved, however, make such mortgages more risky for all but the most financially sophisticated borrower.

SCHOOL FEES

Over the past ten years there has been a significant increase in the demand for places at independent schools. Annual fees at independent schools can be quite substantial:

School	Age	Fees
Primary Level		
Pre - Prep	2/7 years	£300 - £600 per term
Day School	7/13 years	£500 - £1,900 per term
Boarding School	7/13 years	£1,100 - £2,750 per term
Second Level		
Day School	13/18 years	£1,100 to £3,500 per term
Boarding School	13/18 years	£1,600 to £4,000 per term

POST-A LEVELS EDUCATION

Universities

There are 54 autonomous universities in the UK, each of which:
- administers its own budget
- awards its own degrees
- makes its own rules.

Courses are usually highly academic and last for at least three years. University Science/Engineering Faculties now tend to have strong links with industry.

Polytechnics

There are 30 polytechnics in the UK all of which are funded by Local Education Authorities. Degree courses are standardised and awarded by C.N.A.A. (Council of National Academic Awards).

Polytechnics offer:
- A wide variety of degree and non-degree and post-graduate courses.
- A course-range that is now increasing to include traditional university-type subjects.
- Professional and vocational-type courses e.g. Aeronautical Engineering, Accounting, Catering Studies etc.

HIGHER EDUCATION FEES

L.E.A. (Local Education Authority) grants are available for over 18s and comprise tuition fees and maintenance grants. Entitlement to a maintenance grant is assessed on the basis of parental income. Such grants can be mandatory or discretionary.

Mandatory grants are payable in respect of designated courses and were frozen in 1990. In the November 1993 budget the Chancellor speeded up the process of transferring higher education costs from the state to the students by reducing these grant payments by 10% in 1994 and by similar amounts in 1995 and 1996. Future cost-increases and grant reductions will be financed by student loans.

Your eligibility for a discretionary grant is decided by the L.E.A. and if you are successful it will usually be at the same level as a mandatory grant.

SCHOOL FEES

For parents wishing to educate their children privately, funding school fees can be a major problem, if some degree of planning is not undertaken in advance.

Drawing up a plan can be quite onerous, as there are a number of factors which can be quite difficult to evaluate. The following points may give you some ideas as you set about making this evaluation.

- What is the current level of fees payable at the school of your choice?
- What period of time will elapse before the first fees become due?
- Over what period of time will these fees be payable?
- What is your estimated annual rate of increase in these fees?
- How many children will you need to provide for?
- What are your own financial prospects over the period?
- Will anyone else help e.g. a grandparent?

Saving in Advance

The most cost-effective way of providing for your family's education is to plan well-ahead. The extent of planning required is illustrated in the following example:

John and Elizabeth have two children Sarah aged 4 and William aged 6. Both will be starting junior shcool at age 7 and then senior school from age 11 to 18. The current fees assumed at the junior school are £3,240 p.a. and at senior school £4,320 p.a. The rise in school fees is assumed at 8% p.a.

Estimated Fees Payable (£)

Year	William	Sarah
1996	3,500	-
1997	3,780	-
1998	4,080	4,080
1999	4,400	4,400
2000	5,880	4,760
2001	6,350	5,140
2002	6,850	6,850
2003	7,400	7,400
2004	8,000	8,000
2005	8,600	8,600
2006	9,300	9,300
2007	10,000	10,000
2008	-	10,800
2009	-	11,660
Total	78,140	90,990

In an earlier section of this guide you will find details on saving and investment mechanisms you may consider appropriate to building a fund suitable for your children's education over a number of years.

Capital Sum Investments for School Fees

Here there are two basic considerations:

- Investment medium
- Who actually owns the money being invested

PARENTAL CAPITAL SUM

If you are a parent and you personally own the lump sum being invested for your children's education, care should be taken to minimise the tax implications, as any income generated by the investment could be considered your income for tax-purposes.

Charitable Trust Schemes

Under these schemes, parents can pay a lump sum into a charitable trust which has been specially-created for their children's education.

The trust may purchase an annuity from a life assurance company which will pay fees over a selected period from the trust fund directly to the school. Because the trust has charitable status, it can reclaim any tax deducted from the annuity payments and thus give you a better return on your investment.

There are two varieties of charitable trust schemes, guaranteed annuity schemes and investment annuity schemes.

Guaranteed Annuity Schemes

Under a guaranteed annuity, each annuity payment is fixed in advance.

In the following table, we illustrate the approximate investment required to produce £1,500 per term for 15 terms (total payments £22,500) in a typical guaranteed annuity scheme.

When Investments are Made	Approx. Investment	Approx. Saving
	£	£
On Starting School	19,000	3,500
4 years before fees commence	12,600	9,900
8 years before fees commence	8,400	14,100
13 years before fees commence	4,900	17,600

Investment Annuity Schemes

Where your capital is invested in a unit-linked fund, the amount of fees paid depends on the investment-performance of the fund between the date of investment to the date the fees become payable. When fees become due, your unit-linked fund is used to purchase an annuity and thus pay the fees on the agreed basis.

OTHER CAPITAL LUMP SUMS

If a capital sum is being provided by a grandparent or other relative, it may be worth setting up a non-charitable trust for the child. The advantage of this is that any income from such a trust would be taxed as the child's own income and would be tax-free up to the normal personal allowance, £3,525 in the 1995/96 tax year.

Personal Pensions

If you are eligible to contribute to a personal pension, you could consider using the plan to finance school fees. Personal pension benefits may be taken from age 50.

Full tax relief is allowed on the contributions to a personal pension fund and, remember, all your personal pension plan contributions do not have to mature at the same time. You could have your main pension contract maturing at age 65 and a subsidiary contract maturing at age 50 to pay school fees.

Up to 25% of a personal pension plan may be taken in a tax-free lump sum and the balance taken in the form of an annuity.

Borrowing

If school fees cannot be funded from your current income or savings, then a loan plan may be your only option.

Many loan plans for school fees work on the basis that a fixed sum is lent each term; you pay interest at a variable rate on the amount outstanding, which may increase progressively until your child leaves school. No tax relief is allowed on interest payments.

Another option might be moving house, remortgaging your home or a grandparent might consider a home income plan. A home income plan may be tax-efficient if the grandparent is over 65, as tax relief can be obtained on such loans, up to £30,000. 90% of home income loans must be used to buy an annuity and the balance may be used for any other purpose.

FAMILY PROTECTION

A most important aspect of financial planning is to protect your family against the financial consequences of your untimely disability or death . This protection may take many forms but will probably be provided by a combination of the following:

- State Benefits
- Pension Benefits
- Life Assurance
- Disability Assurance
- Home Income Plans

STATE BENEFITS

Here, we outline a number of state benefits that can be claimed in the event of your premature death or disability.

Widow's Payment

This is a lump sum of £1,000 payable to a widow on the death of her husband if she is under 60. It is non-taxable.

Widowed Mother's Allowance

This is payable after the Widow's Payment and will cease if you remarry. The benefit is £59 per week from April 1995, with an increase of £11.00 per week for each qualifying child. Any additional (SERPS) pension earned by your late husband may also be paid. These benefits are taxable.

Widow's Pension

This is a flat-rate pension payable if a widow is over 45 and under 60 when her husband dies or when her widowed mother's allowance ceases. Any additional (SERPS) pension earned by the late husband will also be paid. The pension is £59 per week from April 1995 if you are over 55; reduced widow's pension rates are paid if you are 45 to 54. This benefit is taxable.

Statutory Sick Pay

Most employees are entitled to statutory sick pay from their employers for the first eight weeks when absent from work as a result of illness or disability.

Sickness Benefit

Sickness benefit is payable if you are not entitled to statutory sick pay or if you have exceeded your eight weeks statutory sick-pay period. Your entitlement depends on your national insurance contribution record, unless you were injured at work. The benefit is payable for 28 weeks.

Invalidity Benefit

This is payable after your sickness benefit has expired, if you are still unfit to work. It consists of a pension of £59 per week from April 1995, with increases for dependants and may also be increased by an earnings-related additional (SERPS) pension. There is a further allowance which is age-related.

Industrial Disablement Benefit

This is available for any disablement suffered at work and is paid in addition to sickness and invalidity benefits. Disability does not have to be permanent but does have to last for at least 15 weeks from the original injury, even if it does not prevent the claimant from working. The amount and form of the benefit varies according to the degree of disability. It can be a lump sum or weekly pension.

EMPLOYEE PENSIONS

Employee pension plans can provide family protection under four headings:
- Life Cover
- Early Retirement due to ill health
- Spouse's/Dependent's Pension
- Permanent Health Insurance

Life Cover

The general rule is that the maximum lump sum paid in the event of your death cannot be greater than four times your final pensionable salary. However, for schemes set up on or after 14th March 1989, or if you joined a scheme on or after 1st June 1989, there is also an overall cash limit. In the 1995/96 tax year, this limit is £314,400. Remember, life insurance payable from previous pension plans also counts towards this limit. Your own personal pension contributions may also be paid as a lump sum in the event of your death (this will not apply to your employer's contributions).

Early Retirement due to ill health

You do not have to be completely incapable of work to take advantage of early retirement provisions of many pension schemes. So, if your health is sufficiently bad as to prevent you from pursuing your normal occupation, or seriously reducing your earning capability, you may retire at any age, provided your individual pension scheme allows for it.

Remember, many employee schemes set limits on the benefits payable on early retirement due to ill health and these may be considerably less than those allowed by the Inland Revenue.

Example:

William is 55 and is considering early retirement. His normal retirement age is 65. William has been working with his current employer for the last 15 years, his salary is £40,000 p.a.

If William retires early because of ill health, the maximum pension and cash tax-free lump sum allowed by the Inland Revenue are as follows:
- Pension 40/60 x £40,000 = £26,667 a year or
- Lump Sum 120/80 x £40,000 = £60,000 and a reduced pension

NOTE: If William was seriously ill with a short life expectancy, the total pension fund could be paid in one lump sum, less a 20% tax on the amount in excess of £60,000.

Spouse's Pension

The general rule is a spouse's pension, not greater than two-thirds of the maximum pension you could have received may be payable. "Maximum" means the maximum in accordance with the Inland Revenue rules and is calculated in accordance with your current salary and the number of years service you would have had at normal retirement. If your pension plan was set up on or after the 14th March 1989, or if you joined on or after 1st June 1989, there is also a maximum on a spouse's pension of £34,933 (two-thirds of £52,400) in the 1995/96 tax year; this limit is normally adjusted each year to take account of inflation.

Dependent's Pension

A dependent's pension may also be paid to one or more of your dependents, other than your spouse, up to a maximum of 2/3rds of your retirement pension.

A pension for a dependent child ceases when the child stops being dependent, i.e. reaches the age of 18 or finishes full-time education. Other dependents' pensions may continue indefinitely.

A spouse's pension and dependent's pension when added together cannot exceed the maximum pension benefits you could have had.

Permanent Health Insurance

Now many permanent health insurance contracts are sold as part of a group pension plan. If the scheme is approved by the Inland Revenue, premiums paid by your employer will not count as part of your remuneration for income-tax purposes. However, if you personally contribute to a Permanent Health Insurance scheme you will not be allowed tax relief on the contributions.

Income received under a group permanent health insurance plan paid for by your employer will be taxed under PAYE.

PERSONAL PENSION PLANS

Life Cover

Under a personal pension plan, you can buy life assurance cover with up to 5% of your net relevant earnings and get full tax relief at your relevant tax rate.

Life cover under an old-style retirement annuity is called a Section 226A policy; the new-style personal pension plan is known as a Section 637 policy.

The approximate amount of life cover you could buy with 5% of net relevant earnings (NRE) to age 60 is outlined on page 50 assuming normal conditions apply.

Net Relevant Earnings p.a.	£10,000	£25,0000	£50,000
Age	Amount of Life Cover	Amount of Life Cover	Amount of Life Cover
25	£280,000	£725,500	£1,450,000
40	£117,000	£300,000	£600,000
50	£67,500	£173,000	£350,000

Dependent/Pension

Under a personal plan, you can arrange for a pension to be paid to your spouse, your children and other dependents in the event of your premature death. If your personal pension plan does not include any arrangement for paying pensions to your dependents, a lump sum which is equivalent to the amount of your accumulated fund may be paid, or your contributions to the relevant date together with reasonable interest may be paid.

Under an old-style retirement annuity plan, the amount of the pension payable is determined by the amount of money in your pension fund.

Under the new-style personal pension plan, the total pension for dependents cannot exceed the retirement pension which the fund would have yielded if you could have retired at the date of your death.

LIFE ASSURANCE

Life assurance is a very complex area. Here, we give a brief outline of the contracts available and some background information.

The simplest form of life assurance is term assurance. How much you pay for term assurance will not only depend on the sum assured but also on a number of other factors such as:

- your age
- your lifestyle
- your general state of health
- the options included in the policy
- the term of the policy.

Your Age

As you get older the cost of life assurance increases. Because their life expectancy is greater, rates for women are cheaper than those for men. The rates for women are generally equivalent to those for men three or four years younger.

Approximate costs of providing a ten-year term assurance plan of £100,000 on a male non-smoker for 10 years are set out below:

Age	Annual Cost
30	£185
45	£450
55	£1,100

Your Lifestyle

Believe it or not, your lifestyle may also dramatically affect your life assurance costs. For example, premium rates paid by non-smokers are normally cheaper than those for smokers. A non-smoker's age is equivalent to that of a smoker three to four years younger. For younger lives, foreign travel and marital status may also be relevant factors, due to the ever-increasing health risks.

General State of Health

Obviously, your general state of health is important from the life assurance company's point of view. If you are suffering from a serious illness, you may be unable to obtain any life assurance cover at all or you may be 'loaded'. e.g. a 50% loading would mean you pay 50% more than the average insured person for the same age for the same amount of life cover.

Policy Options

Many term-assurance plans now include policy options. These options may, for example, allow you to increase your sum assured or to change your plan during its term to a whole of life or an endowment assurance plan without further medical evidence. You pay extra for these options.

Term of the Policy

The chart below illustrates the natural risk of death.

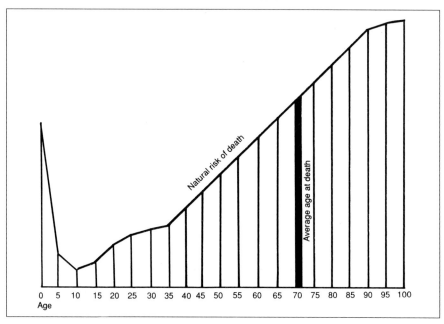

Term Assurance

When you take out a term assurance plan, you agree to pay a specific or level premium over an agreed number of years. Each year your risk of death increases so a level premium is based on the average risk.

In the early years of the plan you pay too much, as is illustrated in the chart on page 53. The chart is based on a level premium term assurance plan over 30 years, for a non-smoking male, commencing at age 30.

That part of each premium which is not required in the early years to cover the actual life assurance costs is invested by the life assurance company in a 'surplus fund'. This fund is used to cover your extra life assurance costs in later years. If you live to age 60 everything is fine; however, in the event of your plan being discontinued or in the event of an early claim, no part of this 'surplus fund' is repaid to you by the life assurance company.

Many life assurance plans now avoid the creation of this surplus fund and thus give more equitable benefits to everyone.

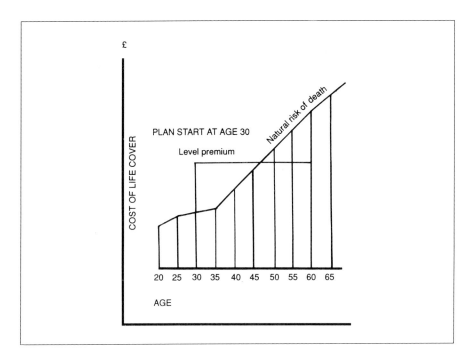

Flexible Unit-Linked Assurance

With flexible unit-linked assurance plans you agree to pay premiums on a regular basis over a number of years. Each month your premiums are invested in units in the life assurance company's investment portfolio, at whatever the Unit Price is at that time. Also, each month, a number of units are sold back to the life assurance company to pay for your life assurance cover and management expenses.

If your units perform exactly in accordance with assumed growth rates, the sum assured will be maintained to the end of the term of the policy. If the units perform better, there will be a cash value in the policy which you can take at the end of the term. If the units perform at a lower rate than that assumed premiums will have to be increased or the sum assured reduced.

Guaranteed Unit-Linked Assurance

On a guaranteed policy, premiums are fixed at the outset and you buy a fixed sum assured, payable on death, for a specific term. If the units do not perform, your life cover continues and the life company suffers a loss. If the units do better than expected, then the value of the units left in the policy at the end of the term is payable to you.

53

Renewal Term Assurance

Some term assurances are 'renewable' in that, on the expiry date, there is an option to take out further term assurance at normal rates without evidence of health. Each subsequent policy will usually have this same option. Thus, instead of purchasing a 20-year term assurance, you could effect a five-year renewable term assurance. At renewal, your new premiums may be substantially more as they will be based on your age at the date of renewal.

Convertible Term Assurance

This is a level term assurance with an option which enables you to convert it at any time during its term into a whole of life or an endowment assurance plan, without any further medical evidence. The premium payable at conversion will normally be that applicable to your age at the date of conversion to a whole of life or endowment assurance.

The premiums payable for convertible term assurance will be higher than those payable for ordinary term assurance plans.

Decreasing Term Assurance

Under a decreasing term assurance plan, the sum assured reduces each year by a stated amount. It is normally used to cover borrowings, such as home mortgages.

Although the cover decreases each year, the premium will remain constant. However, decreasing term assurance is normally payable over a shorter period than the term of the loan.

Increasing Term Assurance

Here, the sum assured can be increased each year by a set percentage of the original sum assured or can be renewed at the end of the term, for a higher amount. For example, if you have a five-year increasing term assurance plan you could have the option to renew the policy with a 50% increase in the sum assured at the end of the term without evidence of health.

Family Income Policies

A family income plan is designed to provide a fixed lump sum by instalments for a selected period of time. The policy pays the lump sum each year from the date of your death until the expiry date of the policy. The annual lump sum may be paid at monthly or quarterly intervals.

These policies are relatively cheap, as the overall sum at risk, from the life assurance company's point of view, decreases each year over the term of the policy if no claim is made.

Dread Disease or Critical Illness Cover

This type of life assurance cover is relatively new, the sum assured is paid on the diagnosis of what is called a Dread Disease. The main advantage of this type of plan is that the sum assured is paid before your death.

The policy will define what a "Dread Disease" is and normally includes strokes, coronary artery disease, heart attacks, kidney failure, major organ transplants and paralysis. However, a dread disease payment is normally an alternative, not an addition, to the sum assured on death. Thus, if a payout is made on the diagnosis of a dread disease, no further payment may be made on your subsequent death.

Whole-Life Policies

A whole-life policy pays out a sum assured whenever you die and is not restricted to a specific term as in the case of conventional term assurance.

A standard whole-life policy has a level premium, payable throughout your life and it pays a fixed sum, whenever your death occurs. Some whole-of-life assurance plans offer a cessation of premium payments on attainment of a certain age, say 80 or 85; these contracts are normally more expensive as premiums will on average be payable over a shorter term of years.

OTHER CONSIDERATIONS

When you decide to commence a new life assurance protection plan, consideration should be given to certain legal formalities on the framework of the new plan. Before we go into this framework let us clarify three simple points:

- Life Assured: The person on the duration of whose life the life assurance policy depends.

- The Assured: (Grantee) The person or party entitled to receive the proceeds of the policy on the death of the life assured.

  Insurance Interest: An insurable interest is necessary in every life insurance contract. You have an unlimited insurable interest in your own life and that of your spouse. In other cases you will normally have to substantiate your financial interest in the life of another person before a life assurance company will insure that life for your benefit.

Own Life Policies

If a policy is what is called an 'own life' plan i.e. you are both the life assured and the assured, so the lump sum payable on your death will form part of your estate when you die, this may give rise to two problems.

- the policy proceeds may be subject to inheritance tax
- the life office cannot pay out the policy proceeds until your legal personal representatives can produce their grant of representation and proof of title.

This may delay payment for many months. If you did not make a will the proceeds of the policy will be distributed according to the law of intestacy, see page 127. This may not be in accordance with your final wishes.

Joint-Life Policies

In many families, nowadays, both spouses contribute financially to the family budget, so it may be cost-effective to consider a joint life policy. Joint-life policies on husband and wife normally pay the survivor on the death of the first to die. Joint-life policies have no inheritance-tax implications for married couples.

Life of Another

Under a life of another policy, the assured is someone other than the life assured. Because the policy belongs to the assured, it is not part of the 'life assured's estate on death. The proceeds are thus not subject to inheritance tax and the assured may claim payment swiftly by producing the policy document and proof of death. One disadvantage of this type of contract is that, should your personal circumstances change, you have no control over the policy - other than to stop paying the premiums.

Trusts

Many family-protection plans are now written in trust. Plans written under trust have the following advantages:

- The plan is not part of your estate when you die and thus not subject to inheritance tax. Premiums paid will be transfers for inheritance-tax purposes, if they are not exempt under the annual exemption limits.
- Payment is quick and easy because the life office will pay the surviving trustee(s) on proof of death and the production of the policy document.
- You can maintain a degree of control over the policy during your lifetime by being a trustee for the policy yourself.

Having your family-protection plan written in trust is easy: you simply request the life assurance company to do so, before you commence a plan. You do this by completing a standard trust form, nominating the trustee(s) and the beneficiaries.

PERMANENT HEALTH INSURANCE

Permanent health insurance (PHI) differs from life assurance in that its benefits are payable when you are sick or injured and not on death. It is intended as a substitue for earned income that is displaced by sickness or injury.

Costs

PHI costs vary with age, sex, occupation and deferred period. As you get older, the chances of being disabled increase and so premiums increase. Females, on average, suffer more ill-health than males and thus pay higher premiums.

Occupation is also a crucial factor. First, because some occupations carry a higher risk of disability due to accidents and illness than others. Secondly, it is easier to return to work with some degree of incapacity in some occupations than it is in others.

The longer the period of deferrment, the cheaper the premiums. The standard deferred periods are 4, 13, 26 and 52 weeks.

Some PHI plans offer a no-claims discount. So, if you do not make a claim, say in the first three years, you get a 20% discount on premiums paid from the fourth year onwards.

Limitation of Benefits

In order to ensure that you are not better-off financially by claiming benefit, many plans put a limit on benefits payable. These limits will be operated regardless of the benefit insured. A normal limitation is that the total monthly disability benefit payable to you cannot exceed three-quarters of your average earnings in the year prior to disablement. Most plans also include state disability benefits and employers sick-pay within this 75% rule.

Tax

If you effect a PHI plan, you get no tax relief on the premiums and the benefits are taxed as unearned income. However, due to a concession agreed with the Inland Revenue, benefits are not taxed until they have been received for one complete tax year. Thus, the exact period during which payments can be paid tax-free depends on the time of year when your disability payments commence; the maximum tax-free period being two years less one day.

"The lure of the distant and difficult is deceptive. The great opportunity is where you are now."

John Burroughs

PART TWO

PENSIONS

Nobody wants financial headaches after a lifetime of hard work. In the following pages, we give a broad outline of various avenues available to you now in planning your pension, together with one or two ways of securing your financial future in a tax-efficient way.

PENSIONS

In the last fifty years, average life expectancy has increased by no less than twenty years. The average man retiring at the age of 65 can now look forward to a further 14 to 17 years in retirement. The average woman, since women tend to live longer, can look forward to 17 to 20 years.

This raises the question of what are you going to live on, once you have completed your active working-life? The answer is generally simple- 'A PENSION'.

However, the subject of pensions is one which many people are happier to ignore while they are working and in particular during their early working lives. Regardless of your present attitude towards pensions, a pension is something for which you must plan well in advance. You cannot simply wait until you need it: by then it will be too late. Here, we outline the very least you need to know about the whole subject of pensions.

Basically, there are three kinds of pension income in retirement:-

- National Insurance Pensions
- Employee Pensions
- Personal Pensions

Many people receive retirement benefits from a combination of these sources. In fact, it seems prudent not to rely entirely on any one, and a degree of diversification of retirement income seems best in most cases.

Planning your own pension to add to whatever other pension benefits you may be entitled to is also a good idea, especially when you consider that the Inland Revenue will be happy to help you pay for it.

NATIONAL INSURANCE PENSIONS

There are two main National Insurance or State pensions: the Basic Pension and the State Earnings-Related Pension Scheme (SERPS), also known as the 'additional' pension. Your National Insurance contributions determine the size of your state pensions.

NATIONAL INSURANCE (NI) CONTRIBUTIONS

There are four different contribution classes.

Class 1	Class 1 contributions are paid by employees whose earnings exceed the Lower Earnings Limit; (£59 per week in the 1995/96 tax year). You pay Class 1 NI contributions on earnings up to the Upper Earnings Limit, (£440 per week in the current tax year). Your employer pays Class 1 NI contributions on all your earnings.
	There are different rates of Class 1 NI contributions; which one you pay depends on your earnings and on whether you are contracted in or out of SERPS.
	Some married women and widows pay Class 1 NI contributions at a special reduced-rate.
Class 2	If you are in self-employment, you pay Class 2 NI contributions at a single flat rate (£5.85 per week in the 1995/96 tax year), if profits from your business are below a certain limit, you may decide not to pay Class 2 contributions.
Class 3	If you have gaps in your NI contributions record you can volunteer to pay Class 3 contributions, (£5.75 per week in the 1995/96 tax year), and make good any gaps in your contributions over the past six years.
Class 4	If you are self-employed with profits between certain limits, (£6,640 and £22,880 for current year), you pay Class 4 NI contributions at 7.3% of income within these limits.

BASIC NI PENSION

You are normally entitled to claim a Basic NI Pension if you satisfy the following conditions:

- have reached State Pension Age, which is 65 for a man and 60 for a woman.
- have paid, or been credited with, sufficient National Insurance contributions.

CLASS 1 - NATIONAL INSURANCE CONTRIBUTION RATES

1995/96

Earnings Per Week	EMPLOYEE					EMPLOYER		
	Not Contracted out of SERPS		Contracted out of SERPS		Reduced Rate	Not Contracted Out of SERPS	Contracted Out of SERPS	
	First £57	Bal	First £57	Bal			First £57	Bal
Under £59	0%	0%	0%	0%	0%	0%	0%	0%
£59 to £104.99	2%	10%	2%	8.2%	3.85%	3.0%	3.0%	0%
£105 to £149.99	2%	10%	2%	8.2%	3.85%	5.0%	5.0%	2.0%
£150 to £204.99	2%	10%	2%	8.2%	3.85%	7.0%	7.0%	4.0%
£205 to £440	2%	10%	2%	8.2%	3.85%	10.2%	10.2%	7.2%
Balance	0%	0%	0%	0%	0%	10.2%	10.2%	10.2%

CONTRIBUTION CONDITIONS The amount of Basic Pension payable depends on your National Insurance contribution-record over your working life; which is normally 49 years for a man and 45 years for a woman.

Your working life normally begins with the start of the tax year in which you were aged 16, and ends in the tax year in which you attain State Pension Age.

The state pension age for women will be raised on a phased basis to age 65 over a 10 year period beginning in year 2010. This measure will affect all women currently under 45 years of age.

FULL BASIC PENSION You may claim the full Basic Pension if you satisfy the following two conditions:

- If you have paid Class 1, 2 or 3 NI contributions of at least 52 times the weekly Lower Earnings Limit in any tax year.
- If NI Contributions were paid or credited to you for approximately 90% of your working life. A reduced pension is payable for a shorter contribution history, the minimum pension being 25% of the full rate. Examples of this reduction are as follows:

Number of Qualifying Years	Percentage of the full basic pension for which you qualify	
	Women	Men
9 or less	0	0
10	26	0
11	29	25
15	39	35
20	52	46
30	77	69
39	100	89
44 or more	100	100

The present system of basic pensions started on 5th July 1948. If you were already 16 on that date, the system could work unfairly against you. So, special rules exist which can enhance your basic pension by reducing the length of your working life and, thus, the number of years you need in order to qualify for the maximum level of pension.

MARRIED WOMEN As a married woman, you can qualify for a Basic Pension in one of two ways:

- by satisfying the contribution conditions on your own record.

- by reference to your husband's contributions, if he is in receipt of a pension and if you are over 60 years of age . Your rate of pension will be approximately 60% of your husband's basic pension.

HOME-RESPONSIBILITIES PROTECTION If you are unable to qualify for the Basic Pension due to the years you spent at home caring for certain dependents, contribution credits may be given for each complete tax year after 1978 assuming:

- Child benefit was paid for a child under 16 years of age and you were the main payee claiming home-responsibilty protection.

- You regularly spent at least 35 hours a week looking after someone who is over 16 and who had been getting a constant attendance-allowance.

- You have been getting supplementary benefit in order to look after an elderly or sick person at home.

This protection benefit is not available in any tax year where you paid reduced National Insurance contributions.

FULL-YEAR CONTRIBUTIONS Since 6th April 1975, only a full-year's contribution counts towards the Basic Pension. However, you can build up a Basic Pension entitlement with a mixture of different classes of NI contributions in any tax year. If you have paid Class 1 NI contributions for part of a year, you may buy Class 3 contributions for the remainder of that year. You can also make good any gaps over the last six years by paying Class 3 NI contributions.

STATE BASIC-PENSION RATES

Year		Single Person	Married Couple
1995/96		3,075.80	4,911.40
1994/95		2,995.20	4,789.20
1993/94		2,917.20	4,669.60
1992/93		2,815.80	4,508.40
1991/92		2,704.00	4,329.00
1990/91		2,438.80	3,905.20

You can defer your basic pension for up to five years. If you do so, the pension eventually payable to you will be increased by 7.5% p.a. for each year which you deferred. Your Basic Pension will automatically become payable at age 65 for women and age 70 for men. So, you cannot defer your pension for more than five years.

STATE EARNINGS-RELATED PENSION SCHEMES (SERPS)

If you are working for an employer, you can build up State Earnings-Related Pension (SERPS) by paying Class 1 NI contributions at the full rate.

Each week that you pay Class 1 NI contributions on earnings above the lower earning limit you are adding to your SERPS pension. So, you do not need a complete year's contributions to commence building a SERPS Pension, as in the case of the Basic Pension.

The amount of your SERPS pension depends on your 'surplus earnings' in the years during which you have paid full Class 1 NI contributions. Surplus earnings are worked out as follows:

- annual earnings after 6th April 1978 are adjusted up to retirement, in line with the national average earnings index.

- each adjusted annual earnings figure at retirement is reduced by the lower earnings limit applicable to that tax year in which you are aged 64 for a man, and 59 for a woman. This net amount is called your 'surplus earnings'.

Your SERPS pension is then calculated as a fraction of your total surplus earnings:

- if you retire on or before the 5th April 1998, the fraction is one-eightieth of each year's surplus earnings. Since there will be a maximum of 20 years' contributions by 1998, the maximum SERPS pension will be equivalent to approximately one quarter (20 x 1/80) of your average surplus earnings between the Lower and Upper Earnings Limits.

- if you retire after the 5th April 1998, the maximum SERPS pension will be gradually reduced over ten years, falling to approximately a fifth of relevant surplus earnings by 2008.

Example:

Charles retired in May 1994 at age 65 after paying Class 1 National Insurance contributions for 10 years.

In the table on page 66 Column 2 gives the SERPS upper carnings limit for each relevant tax year.

Charles earnings for SERPS pension purposes are as outlined in Column 3.

Column 4 gives the relevant revaluation factors.

Column 5 gives Charles's revalued earnings.

Column 6 gives surplus earnings, i.e. Charles's revalued earnings less the lower earnings limit for 1993/94 of £56 per week or £2,913 per annum.

Tax Year	Upper Earnings Limit	Charle's Earnings	Revaluation Factor	Revalued Earnings	Surplus Earnings
1984/85	13,000	12,000	97.6%	23,712	20,799
1985/86	13,780	14,000	85.4%	25,548	22,635
1986/87	14,820	15,000	70.3%	25,238	22,325
1987/88	15,340	16,000	58.6%	24,329	21,416
1988/89	15,860	17,000	45.8%	23,124	20,211
1989/90	16,900	17,000	32.1%	22,325	19,412
1990/91	18,200	17,500	23.1%	21,543	18,630
1991/92	20,280	19,000	11.8%	21,242	18,329
1992/93	21,060	20,000	5.0%	21,000	18,087
1993/94	21,840	21,000	-	21,000	18,087
Total Surplus Earnings					£199,931

Charles's SERPS pension is calculated as follows:

£199,931 ÷ 80 = £2,499 p.a. or £48.06 p.w.

RETIREMENT After your retirement, your SERPS pension will increase in line with inflation. There are also rules which allow for a widow to inherit part of her husband's SERPS pension. A widower can also inherit part of his wife's SERPS pension if she was over 60, and he over 65, at the time of her death.

DEFERRED PENSION On reaching pensionable age, you can defer claiming your SERPS pension; additional pension benefits will acrue at a rate of 7.5% p.a. for each full year deferred as in the case of the basic pension.

The maximum period of deferral is five years. No additional NI contributions are payable by you during this five year period.

INVALIDITY PENSION

If you are temporarily ill, you may qualify for statutory sick pay or sickness benefit. If you are still ill after 28 weeks and you have paid the appropriate National Insurance contributions, you will be transferred to the longer-term invalidity benefit.

Invalidity Benefit is made up of a number of segments:

Invalidity Pension - This is the basic invalidity benefit, and equivalent in value to the basic pension.

Additional Invalidity Pension - This is an earnings-related benefit paid in addition to the basic invalidity pension. It is based on your paid Class 1 National Insurance Contributions. Additional invalidity benefit has now been phased out and no new entitlements can be build up after 6th April 1991. However, entitlements before 6th April 1991 will continue to be payable.

Invalidity Allowance - is an extra payment that you may receive if you were under the age of 60 (men) or 55 (women) when your illness commenced.

DIVORCE

If your marriage ends in divorce before you reach state pension age and you do not remarry, you can qualify for a basic pension based on your own or your former husband's contributions. You can also use your former husband's National Insurance record to qualify for the basic pension if your marriage ends after you have reached state pension age.

WIDOW'S BENEFITS   Your National Insurance benefits in the event of your husband's death are dependant on:
-   your husband's age at date of death
-   your age at date of your husband's death
-   whether or not you have dependant children.

The benefit payable may include some or all of the following:
-   Widow's Payment
-   Widowed Mother's Allowance and a SERPS pension
-   A Widow's Pension and a SERPS Pension.

Your widow will receive the widow's payment provided she is under 60 and you were not receiving or eligible for a basic retirement pension. If you have dependent children - i.e. children for whom she can claim child benefit, she will also be eligible for the widowed mother's allowance. The widowed mother's allowance will normally be paid for as long as she is caring for the dependent children or until she remarries.

If your widow is under 45 at the date of your death and you have no dependent children she may only qualify for the widow's payment. If your widow is aged 45 or over at the date of your death and you have no dependent children she can claim the widow's pension.

The full widows and SERPS pensions are payable to widows aged 55 or over. However, women who were younger than this when first widowed or on the date when your children cease to be dependent children, will be paid reduced pensions.

WIDOWERS

There are no formal national insurance benefits for widowers. However, if you have dependent children you can claim child benefit and also qualify for single parent benefit.

GRADUATED PENSION This is another State Earnings-Related Pension Scheme which ran from the 6th April 1961 to the 5th April 1975 for people earning over £9 a week at that time. If you belonged to it, every £9 you contributed if you are a woman, and every £7.50 you contributed if you are a man, counts as one 'unit'. In the current year, each unit you hold buys you 7.48p graduated pension per week. The maximum graduated pension you can get in the current year is £6.43 per week for a man or £5.39 per week for a woman.

A widow at age 60 can inherit half of her husband's graduated pension; a widower can inherit half of his wife's graduated pension, if he is over 65 and she was over 60 at the date of her death.

Over 80s Pension

If you are aged 80 or over and you are entitled to a NI retirement pension of less than £35.30 a week or no pension at all you may qualify for the over 80s pension provided you have lived in the UK for at least 10 years out of the 20 years since you reached age 60.

CONTRACTING-OUT OF SERPS You may now contract out of SERPS by joining a contracted-out employer's pension scheme or through an appropriate personal pension plan. This means that you will give up part of your SERPS pension at retirement and get a new pension from your alternative pension arrangement. The amount of this pension will depend on the type of scheme you choose and how well your alternative pension fund performs between now and your retirement age.

Final Salary Scheme With an employer's final pay pension scheme, you and your employer pay a lower rate of NI contributions on part of your earnings. Your employer's pension scheme will then guarantee you a minimum pension, broadly equivalent to your SERPS pension at retirement. Your final pension income is then made up of this new guaranteed pension and a reduced SERPS pension. You can never lose by contracting-out in this way - and you will probably gain, as most employers' schemes pay more than the guaranteed amount at retirement.

Money-Purchase With an employer's money-purchase pension scheme you and your employer pay a lower rate of NI contributions on part of your earnings. Your employer pays the contributions so saved into a pension fund to buy you what are called *protected pension rights at retirement*. In effect, this means a pension which increases by a minimum of 3% p.a. and also provides a widow's or widower's pension.

At retirement, your SERPS pension is reduced as if you had been contracted-out through a final salary scheme. Your protected pension rights from the new employer's scheme may be more or it may be less than the reduction in your SERPS pension.

Appropriate Pension Plans (APP) With an appropriate personal pension plan, you and your employer pay the full rate of NI contributions, as if you were contracted into SERPS. The difference between the contracted-in rate and the contracted-out rate is paid by the Government into an *appropriate personal pension* on your behalf: this is known as NI Rebate. This rebate is used to build up a fund to buy you protected pension rights at retirement age. Again, at retirement, your SERPS pension is reduced as if you had been contracted-out through an employer's final pay scheme. Your pension from your appropriate pension plan may be more or it may be less than the reduction in your SERPS pension on retirement.

CHOICES

All employees now have the freedom to contract-out of SERPS. However, only by contracting-out through an employer's final pay pension scheme can you be guaranteed to do at least as well as the SERPS pension which you will be giving up.

There is no such guarantee with any other type of pension arrangement, where the pension you get at retirement depends on how well your contributions are invested, and on the annuity rate prevailing at the date of your retirement.

Younger people will generally do better by contracting-out because their NI contributions have longer to grow and are more likely to build up a bigger pension benefit than the SERPS pension you give up. Men do better than women of the same age, because they tend to retire later and die younger.

ADVICE SERVICE Your NI pension entitlements can get very complicated; happily the Department of Social Security (DSS) operates a Retirement Pension Forecast and Advice (RPFA) service. You can use this service to find out what your pension entitlements are and what your pension is likely to be at retirement. They will also advise you on what you can do now to increase your future State pension entitlements.

The DSS service will give you a forecast on your Basic, SERPS and Graduated Pension. Complete Form BR 19 and return it to the address on the form.

PENSION PLANNING

The Basic State Pension was planned at approximately 25% national average earnings for a single person. SERPS was intended to double this Basic State Pension to approximately 50% of national average earnings. However, these percentages now seem optimistic.

Many benefits normally associated with pension plans are not provided within the National Insurance Scheme.

- A pension for earnings above the upper earnings limit.
- A cash lump sum on your premature death.
- A tax-free lump sum on retirement.
- A pension on early retirement.

So, if you would like your income in retirement to be related in a reasonable way to your pre-retirement income, you should give pension planning priority right now. You can do this through:

- An Employer Pension Scheme
- A Personal Pension Plan.

EMPLOYER PENSION SCHEMES

Although employers are not obliged by law to set up an Employer Pension Scheme, nowadays many employers do so. The Inland Revenue require that where an employer operates a pension scheme on behalf of his/her employees, part of the cost must be paid by the employer; this may explain the reluctance of some employers to set up a pension scheme.

PARTIES TO AN EMPLOYER'S PENSION SCHEME

- The Employer - who must initially agree to set up the scheme and is normally responsible for the major share of the operating costs.
- The Members - the employees covered by the scheme.
- The Trustee(s) - the individual(s) who have the responsibility of collecting contributions, their investment and their eventual repayment as pension benefits.
- The Administrator - the Manager of the pension scheme.
- Superannuation Funds Office (S.F.O.) - party who must approve the scheme for tax purposes.

MEMBERS Under an approved retirement pension scheme most employees liable to pay tax under Schedule E are entitled to become members of a pension scheme. So, membership may include:

- Directors whose income is assessable under Schedule E
- Part-time or temporary employees
- Genuinely employed spouses of professional and self-employed people,
- Salaried but not equity partners in a partnership
- UK-resident employees of overseas employers.

MEMBERSHIP CATEGORIES Occupational pension schemes have undergone many changes in recent years. These changes were brought about mainly by the 1987 Finance Act (No 2) and the 1989 Finance Act. In broad terms, there are three main categories of membership:

Pre-1987 Members: Maximum benefits may be provided under one of these schemes if they were established before the 17th March 1987, and you joined before that date.

1987-1989 Members: Maximum benefits may be provided under one of these schemes if they were established before the 14th March 1989, and you had joined on or after the 17th March 1987 and before the 1st June 1989.

Post-1989 Members: Maximum benefits may be provided under one of these schemes if you joined it after the 1st June 1989, regardless of when the scheme was established. Post-1989 benefits may also be applicable if you joined a scheme before the 1st June 1989, established on or after the 14th March 1989.

MAXIMUM BENEFITS

Maximum pension benefits normally depend on your years of service and your salary at retirement. Generally, under the Inland Revenue rules, the maximum pension which you can receive at your normal retirement age is 2/3rds of your final salary.

FINAL SALARY may be defined as either:

- any one year's emoluments out of the last five before retirement, or
- the average of the best three or more consecutive years' emoluments ending not more than ten years prior to retirement. This definition is obligatory for 20% directors. For schemes set up between the 17th March 1987 and the 14th March 1989, emoluments were limited to £100,000.

EARNING CAP The Finance Act 1989 brought about another change in the definition of 'final salary'. For post-1989 members there is an upper limit of £60,000 in the 1989/90 tax year. This limit is normally adjusted annually in line with increases in the Retail Prices Index and it is £78,600 for the tax year 1995/96.

60th Scale

Many pension schemes provide a pension of 1/60th of final salary for each year of service. So, you get the maximum pension after completing 40 years' service with your employer.

ACCELERATED SCALE (PRE-1987 MEMBERS)

Nowadays, not everybody completes 40 years' service with the same employer. However, if you have completed ten years' service with your employer it is possible for you to receive a pension of 2/3rds of final salary under what is called the Accelerated Scale,

The following table shows how your pension entitlements may be accelerated under the Pre-1987 rules.

Years of Service to normal retirement age	Maximum pension as a fraction of final salary
1 - 5	1/60th for each year
6	8/60ths
7	16/60ths
8	24/60ths
9	32/60ths
10 or more	40/60ths

Accelerated Scale (1987-1989 members and post -1989 members)

If you join a pension scheme on or after the 17th March 1987, or where a new scheme is established on or after that date, the maximum pension is 1/30th of final salary for each year of service.

So, in order to obtain the maximum pension of two-thirds of your final salary you must have completed a minimum of 20 years of service with your employer.

CASH LUMP SUM ON RETIREMENT In exchange for part of your pension, you may take a tax-free cash sum of 3/80ths of final salary for each year of service, up to a maximum of one-and-a-half-times or 120/80ths of your final salary at retirement.

Pre-1987 Members

If you were a member of your pension scheme before the 17th March 1987, it may provide a cash lump sum on an uplifted scale at retirement as follows:

Service (Years)	Maximum 80ths
1- 8	3 for each year
9	30
10	36
11	42
12	48
13	54
14	63
15	72
16	81
17	90
18	99
19	108
20+	120

1987-1989 Members:

If you became a member of a pension scheme during this period, your cash tax-free lump sum is based on 3/80ths of your salary for each year of service, up to a maximum of 120/80ths or one-and-a-half-times your final salary. However, it is possible to provide an additional cash lump sum on the uplifted scale above, provided your pension scheme also provides pension benefits on the accelerated scale i.e. 1/30th of final salary for each year of service.

If your scheme provides a pension between 1/60th and 1/30th of final salary for each year of service, an adjusted uplifted sum may also be paid. This adjusted uplifted sum may generally be calculated in accordance with this formula:

Formula 1	Formula 2
$\dfrac{A - B}{C - B} \times 100 = D$	$E - F \times D = G$

A = Your actual pension
B = Basic Pension based on 60th scale
C = Your maximum pension based on 30th scale
E = Maximum Tax-Free Cash on the uplifted scale
F = Tax-Free Cash based on 3/80ths of final salary for years of service.
G = Uplifted Lump Sum

Example:

Let us assume your service is 20 years, your final salary is £30,000, your actual pension is £18,000.

A = £18,000
B = 20/60ths of £30,000 or £10,000
C = 20/30ths of £30,000 or £20,000
E = Maximum Tax-Free Cash on uplifted scale or 120/80ths of £30,000 or £45,000
F = 3/80ths x 20 or 60/80ths of £30,000 or £22,500.

D is 80% and is calculated as follows:

$$\frac{A - B}{C - B} \times 100 = D \quad OR \quad \frac{£18,000 - £10,000}{£20,000 - £10,000} \times 100 = 80\%$$

G is calculated as follows:

E - F x D i.e. £45,000 - £22,500 x 80% = £18,000

Uplifted lump sum is £18,000

Maximum tax-free lump sum is £40,500 (£22,500 + £18,000).

Post - 1989 Members

The maximum lump sum is the greater of 3/80ths of final salary (subject to restrictions imposed by the 1989 Finance Act) for each year of service, or your maximum pension multiplied by 2.25. An overall limit of £117,900 applies in the 1995/96 tax year.

PENSIONABLE SERVICE Your pensionable service with your current employer is both your future and past service. Any service with a previous employer does not count.

PENSION INCREASES IN RETIREMENT   Your pension in retirement may be increased to reflect the increase in the RPI (Retail Price Index).

However, many pension plans may only provide for pension escalation at a fixed percentage, say 3% or 5% p.a., while others provide for pension increases on a discretionary basis.

NORMAL RETIREMENT AGE The normal retirement age ranges between 60 - 70 for men and 55 - 70 for women. If you are a female director and a 20% shareholder, the normal retirement age is 60 - 70.

EARLY RETIREMENT For schemes set up before the 14th March 1989, you can retire early, subject to your employer's consent after age 50 for men and after age 45 for women, assuming you are within 10 years of Normal Retirement Age.

However, your pension benefits on early retirement will normally be reduced, unless retirement was on the grounds of ill health. Your maximum pension must not exceed one sixtieth of your final pay for each year of service or the maximum pension arrived at by the following formula:

$$\frac{N}{NS} \times P$$

N is the number of actual years service, with a maximum of 40.

P is the maximum pension approval had you remained in service until Normal Retirement Age.

NS is the number of years of potential service to Normal Retirement Age and may be limited to 40.

Post - 1989 Members

The maximum is 1/30th of final remuneration for each year of service completed up to the date of early retirement. Thus, if you have completed twenty years service, a maximum of 2/3rds of final remuneration may be provided from age 50 onwards. For a scheme set up before the 14th March 1989, or if you joined a scheme before the 1st June 1989, you can elect to be covered by the new rules i.e. the new rules applicable to post-March 1989 schemes.

RETIREMENT DUE TO ILL HEALTH   You can retire at any age due to serious ill health without any reduction in pension benefit.

Subject to the consent of the pension trustees and your employer, ill health may be defined as "an incapacity which prevents you from following your normal occupation or seriously impairs your earning-capacity". Full pension and lump sum benefits may be paid on retirement due to ill health, as if you had remained in service up to Normal Retirement Age. Your benefits will be based on your final salary at the date of your retirement.

DEATH-IN-SERVICE BENEFITS If you die before retirement, a cash lump sum of four times pensionable salary at the date of death may be paid. Normally, personal contributions already paid may also be repaid. For post-1989 members, there is an overall cash limit of £314,400 in the 1995/96 tax year and lump sums payable from previous pension plans also count towards this limit.

A cash lump sum and refunds of your personal contributions will normally be paid free of inheritance tax, provided they are distributed at the discretion of the pension fund trustees.

SPOUSE'S PENSION A spouse's pension would be 2/3rds of your maximum-approvable pension, assuming that you continued in employment to Normal Retirement Age with the same final salary as at the date of death. Additional pensions may be paid to other dependents, provided the total of all dependents' pensions would not exceed your pension benefit entitlements.

RETIRING When your retire, your pension can be guaranteed for a fixed period up to 10 years. So, if you die early in retirement your pension may continue to be paid to your estate. If the guaranteed period at the date of death is five years or less, a lump sum equal to the outstanding payments may be paid, instead of continuing with regular pension payments after your death.

BENEFITS ON DEATH AFTER RETIREMENT A pension may be provided for your spouse or dependents should you die in retirement. The maximum spouse's pension is 2/3rds of the maximum-approvable pension which could have been provided for you. Your maximum pension would normally be 2/3rds of your final pensionable salary. So, the maximum spouse's pension will normally be 2/3rds of 2/3rds of your final pensionable salary or 4/9ths of your final pensionable salary.

Where pensions are paid to a widow and one or more dependents, no individual pension can exceed 4/9ths of your final pensionable salary, nor can the aggregate of all the pensions exceed the maximum pension which could have been paid to you.

Widows' or dependents' pensions may increase in line with the RPI, calculated from the date at which you retired, rather than from the time the widow's or dependents' pension commences.

The reduction in the maximum-approvable member's pension for short-serving employees, may also have the effect of reducing dependents' pensions. This will apply to 1987-1989 and post-1989 members.

PAYING FOR A PENSION Paying for your future pension benefits can be very costly, particularly if you wish to fund for the maximum pension benefits allowed within Inland Revenue guidelines. Maximum pension benefits will normally include the following:

- Member's pension: 2/3rds of final pensionable salary at normal retirement age, escalating at up to 8.5% p.a.
- Spouse's pension - Death in Service: 4/9ths of members final pensionable salary escalating at up to 8.5% p.a.
- Spouse's pension - Death in Retirement: 4/9ths of members final pensionable salary escalating at up to 8.5% p.a.
- Life Cover: Four times your pensionable salary.

The chart below illustrates the maximum annual contributions, expressed as a percentage of your pensionable salary, which may be paid into an employer's pension scheme on your behalf, within Inland Revenue guidelines.

Age when Contributions Commenced	Maximum Annual Contribution as % of Salary
30	106%
40	120%
50	148%
60	263%

Major Assumptions:

- Your employer commences making pension contributions at one of the relevant ages.
- You have no 'retained pension benefits' from another scheme.
- You will have 20 years service with your employer at normal retirement age.
- Your salary will escalate at 8.5% p.a. from the date contributions commenced to normal retirement age.
- Pension contributions within the pension fund will grow at 9% p.a.

FUNDING A PENSION A pension fund is normally built up by paying yearly contributions. At retirement age, this fund is used to purchase a pension incorporating all of your retirement benefits. The theory or method used to calculate the size of the yearly contribution necessary to build up this retirement fund is known as the funding method. Generally, one of the following two methods are used:

- Final-Salary or Defined-Benefit Method.
- Money-Purchase or Defined-Contribution Method.

Final-Salary Under this method you are promised a pension which will be related to your salary at retirement. You are usually required to contribute about 5% of salary to the scheme and your employer guarantees you a specific pension at retirement, which is related to your final salary and your years of service. Under this method, there is little or no risk from your point of view, provided your employer's business remains solvent. Your contributions as an employee bear no direct relationship to your eventual pension benefits and as a long-serving employee you will generally get a very good deal. However, if you are an employee who changes jobs often you may not do so well.

Money-Purchase Under this method, the contributions paid by your employer and yourself are defined in advance. The contributions are invested in a pension fund and, when you come to retirement, this accumulated pension fund is used to buy you a pension. The exact amount of pension which your fund will buy is not known until your actual retirement date. So, your final pension is not directly-related to your salary but to the size of your retirement fund and the annuity rates prevailing at the date of your retirement. Thus, your pension fund is directly-related to the amount of contributions paid into the fund over the years and also on how well these contributions were invested. Money-Purchase schemes do not offer employees the same level of security as the Final Salary scheme. However, they can be more attractive to younger employees, particularly if they intend leaving that current employment after a relatively short period.

Transfer-Values The value of your existing pension benefits on changing jobs is known as its transfer-value. In a Final-Salary scheme, the transfer-value is the lump sum that is now required to be invested in a pension fund to buy you your deferred pension entitlements at normal retirement age. In a Money-Purchase scheme, the transfer-value of your pension is the value of units in your pension fund built up by the relevant contributions to the date you left that employment.

CHANGING JOBS

Final salary or defined-benefit schemes are more beneficial for employees who stay a relatively long time, or even all their working life, with the same employer. Employees in Final-Salary schemes who change jobs often can end up with much smaller pensions at retirement. Even with relatively few job changes, your loss of pension benefits can be quite substantial. This is due to the fact that each employer provides a segment of pension benefit related, not to your final salary at retirement age, but, to your final salary when your employment ceased.

Example:

You join employer A at age 30 on a salary of £10,000, at age 40 you change jobs to employer B and at age 50 change again to employer C. All three companies provide pension benefits on 60ths of final salary with a 5% revaluation for deferred benefits. Assuming your salary increases at 8% p.a. throughout your career, at retirement age 60 your pension would be as follows:

Employer	Age on joining	Salary at Leaving or retirement	Deferred Pension	Pensions revalued to retirement age
A	30	£19,990	£3,332	£8,841
B	40	£43,157	£7,193	£11,717
C	50	£93,173	£15,529	£15,529
Total benefits at retirement				£36,080

If you had remained with employer A for your full career, your total pension benefits would have been 30/60ths of £93,173 or £46,586. So, you suffered an annual pension loss of over £10,500 by changing jobs just twice.

Before the Social Security Act 1985, your position would have been substantially worse, as your previous employer(s) would not have been required to provide for the revaluation of your deferred pension. The Social Security Act 1985 requires that deferred pensions based on service after 1st January 1985 be revalued from 1st January 1986 at 5% per annum, or by the increase in the Retail Price Index if this is less.

Money-Purchase Schemes Under a money-purchase scheme you and your employer agree to pay specific contributions to a pension fund. These contributions are normally set as a percentage of your salary. So, when you leave that employment, the transfer-value of your pension is the net worth of these contributions.

When you leave employment with a Money-Purchase pension scheme, you generally have two options:

- leave your existing pension fund in your old employer's scheme; where it will continue to grow and you will eventually get the benefit of the accumulated fund at retirement.
- transfer your existing pension fund to a new employer's scheme, assuming it is authorised to accept it, or to a special personal plan. In either of these funds, your transfer-value will continue to grow until your retirement age.

Refunds If you leave an employer's pension scheme within two years of joining, you can normally get a refund of your contributions. Interest will normally be added to your contributions and tax at the 20% rate will be deducted from the sum refunded.

BUILDING YOURSELF A BETTER PENSION
ADDITIONAL VOLUNTARY CONTRIBUTIONS (AVC)

If you are already in an employer's pension scheme, you may make additional contributions to top-up your benefits at retirement and give yourself a better pension. This mechanism is usually referred to as Additional Voluntary Contributions or AVCS.

Basically, you set up your own Personal Scheme on top of your existing employer's one, and the Inland Revenue do not object, provided your topped-up benefits do not exceed your overall maximum permissible pension benefits.

You may contribute up to 15% of your net relevant earnings in any one tax year and get full tax relief (this 15% does include your existing annual pension contributions).

KNOWING THE RULES At some stage, you were probably given a booklet detailing the rules of your employer's pension scheme. If you do not have one, get hold of one and study it because, as we said earlier, very few private sector pension schemes offer the maximum pension benefits allowed under the Inland Revenue rules.

For instance, the maximum pension you could be provided with is 2/3rds of your final remuneration after 10 or 20 years service, whereas your company's scheme may set out 1/60th of your final remuneration per year of service as your pension entitlement. This means that if you had 25 years service, your final pension from your employer would only be 25/60ths. Quite a bit short of the possible maximum of 20/30ths or 2/3rds! You can use an AVC to bridge this gap.

Again, you might not have provided for a pension for your spouse on your death in retirement. You could use an AVC to provide for such an eventuality.

Your pension might not fully cover you against increases in the cost of living in retirement, a provision for which the Inland Revenue allow. You could normally use an AVC to top-up your pension fund and to increase your pension benefits during your retirement in line with the Retail Price Index.

Another area you may want to provide extra cover for is the loss to you of benefit-in-kind income, like the use of a company car or bonus payments, which are not normally provided for in many pension schemes.

Something worth checking is whether your pension scheme allows you to retire early. It is fine with the Inland Revenue if it does, but many private schemes will penalise you.

Most AVC schemes operate on a Money-Purchase basis, so that the actual level of retirement benefits will not be known until your retirement date. Regular monitoring of AVC funding is important. With many Government and Local Authority pension schemes, AVCs may be used to buy additional years service at retirement; these payments also qualify for tax relief.

Prior to the Finance (No 2) Act 1987, the take-up of AVCs amongst members of company pension schemes was surprisingly low, mainly because of the strict conditions imposed by the Inland Revenue. Contributions, once commenced, had to be continued at existing levels until retirement or for a minimum period of five years, unless genuine financial hardship could be proven. The Finance (No 2) Act 1987 liberalised these conditions. So, from April 1987, the rate and timing at which you can pay AVCs can be varied according to your individual circumstances, provided, of course, the selected scheme allows for this.

AVCs are now far more useful as a tax and financial planning tool, because you can now defer paying AVCs until early April, when your financial position for that particular tax year can be ascertained with high degree of accuracy.

Remember, you can normally only get benefit from an AVC Plan at retirement, unless you leave the scheme within two years of joining, when you can get a refund of your contributions. In these cases, there may be a substantial financial advantage to be gained by paying into an AVC scheme, especially if relief is available to you at the higher rate.

Example:

You are a member of a non-contributory scheme for just under two years. One month before leaving your employer, on the 29th March 1993, you pay 15% of your salary of £40,000 p.a. into an AVC plan and on the 30th April apply for a refund of your contributions.

	£	£
AVC investment	6,000	
Net cost after tax relief at 40%		3,600
20% tax deducted on refund of contributions	1,200	
Refund of contributions	4,800	

You thus have a potential gain of £1,200 on your original net investment of £3,600 over a period of weeks.

Note: Getting this refund may mean you forfeit your rights to any pension benefits from the employer's scheme, something you may regret later in life.

If your AVC is through your employer's scheme, the investment is at the discretion of your employer and the pension trustees. If you wish your AVC contributions to be invested differently to your employer's arranged scheme, for example in unit-linked fund or with a specific pension provider, you can consider a Free-Standing Additional Voluntary Contribution Scheme (FSAVC).

FSAVC

Basically, with a FSAVC you set up your own Personal Scheme on top of your existing employer's one.

Your FSAVC benefits must be aggregated with all other pension benefits in determining the maximum pension permitted by the Inland Revenue and you may not contribute to more than one FSAVC scheme in any one year in respect of the same employment. So, you can have the choice of an AVC scheme arranged in conjunction with your employer's main scheme, or a FSAVC arranged with any recognised pension provider. With a FSAVC, you will probably have a wider choice of investments and more flexible modes of payment. However, an employer's scheme may be more cost-effective, as many employers may pay AVC administration charges under the main scheme, which allows your personal contributions to work much harder for you. Under an FSAVC plan, you usually pay all charges and expenses relating to the new scheme.

TAX RELIEF

Under a FSAVC basic-rate tax relief is given at source and you can claim higher rate tax relief by application to the Inland Revenue through your tax code.

DIVORCE & PENSIONS

As husband and wife you could expect up to two thirds of your spouse's pension if he/she predeceases you, on divorce you may lose your right to this pension.

Structure of many pension schemes makes it virtually impossible to split pension rights equitably between spouses on divorce as pension rights payable some time in the future depend on a variety of factors', for example, will your membership of the scheme continue until retirement? Also pension rights are personal and cannot normally be assigned, even if your spouse has no objection to this.

At present, when a divorce comes before a court, the judge is normally required to take into account the pension rights of each spouse before deciding how other assets are to be allocated. However, where a couple's non-pension assets are limited, this approach may be unsatisfactory.

Further, if as a married woman you opted to pay the married woman's reduced National Insurance Contributions you may also fail to qualify for any State Pension.

PERSONAL PENSION PLANS

Personal Pension Plans or Retirement Annuities are of interest mostly to the self-employed or employees working for an employer who does not operate a group pension scheme.

Before July 1988, personal pension plans were referred to as retirement annuity contracts. The 1987 Finance Act officially introduced Personal Pension Plans from the 1st July 1988, and no new retirement annuity contracts are available after this date. Personal pension plans are in many ways similar to retirement annuity contracts. There are however, some important differences. Normal retirement age for a retirement annuity contract is between 60 and 75, while the normal retirement age for a personal pension plan is between 50 and 75. Also, a personal pension plan may be used to contract-out of SERPS or to accept employer's contributions, while a retirement annuity contract may not.

Basically, Personal Pension Plans are savings plans designed to yield an income on retirement. They normally also incorporate life assurance protection in the event of your premature death. They are particularly attractive because, up to certain limits, contributions to such plans are fully tax-deductible.

PENSION FUND FOR YOUR RETIREMENT In planning a personal pension plan, the idea is to build up a large pension fund during your working life. This fund can then be used to purchase yourself an income or a pension on retirement. A pension fund will normally be made up of two segments:

- Contributions you make during your working life.
- Accumulated profit or growth on these contributions from the date of payment, to the date of retirement.

To a surprisingly large extent, you can decide how you want your contributions invested; so, the type of fund you choose is important. Before choosing a particular fund you should find out:

- how profit or growth on your contributions within the fund are calculated.
- what mechanism the pension provider will use to generate this profit or growth.
- what guarantees, if any, the pension provider will offer you on retirement.
- how the pension provider is paid for his/her services.

FUNDS Personal Pension Plans or retirement annuity contracts can normally be classified under one of the following headings:

Unit-Linked Plans

Jnit-Linked Plans do not normally provide any guaranteed rate of return but, .n the long term, they do stand to offer you a potentially higher rate of return than those offered by many other schemes. Each payment you make is used to purchase units in an authorised pension provider's portfolio of pension investments. The value of the units which you hold is increased by the profits earned on these investments, less management expenses.

Comment: Generally speaking, they are a good investment vehicle over a long period of time.

With-Profit Plans

With-Profit Plans will usually guarantee you a fixed sum at retirement and in addition to this, regular bonuses may be added to this guaranteed sum over the life of the plan. The guaranteed sum is usually small and the bonuses are the non-guaranteed profits earned on the investment of your contributions over the years.

Comment: They are generally seen as being less risky than Unit-Linked plans, and are a solid way of building up a pension fund.

Deposit Account Administration Plans

Deposit Account Administration Plans are, as the name suggests, quite like a building society or a bank deposit account, except that they are operated by an authorised pension provider.

You pay your contributions each year and these contributions, less an agreed amount for management expenses, are credited to your account. Each year, a dividend or profit is declared and this is also credited to your account.

Comment: Secure but in "good times" the long-term potential may be somewhat limited.

RETIRING You can normally retire at any time between the ages 50 and 75 years with a personal pension plan, and between the ages of 60 and 75 for retirement annuities. If you decide to take retirement at normal retirement age or take early retirement due to ill health, you can take up to approximately one quarter of your accumulated fund as a tax-free lump sum, and use the balance to purchase a pension by way of a lifetime annuity. Alternatively, you could decide to use the entire accumulated fund to purchase a bigger lifetime annuity.

The pension or annuity which you choose to buy at retirement can take many forms. It could be level i.e. remaining at the same amount each year from date of retirement to date of your death. Alternatively, it could be *escalating*, which means the annual payments would be increased, by say 5% p.a., each year until your death.

Your pension may be payable monthly, quarterly or annually, whichever you prefer, for the duration of your own life, or for your own life and that of a spouse or dependant relative. It may also be guaranteed for a minimum period of say, 5 or 10, years. It is up to you at retirement age to decide how you wish the pension to be paid. However, once you have decided on the terms under which your future pension will be paid they are extremely difficult if not impossible to alter.

Example:

Eric is 65 years old now and his wife May is 62. They have available £100,000 in Eric's pension fund to buy a pension. The following figures may give you some guidelines on some of the likely pension options available on Eric's retirement.

Type of Pension	Approx. annual pension at date of Purchase
A Level Pension payable for your life annually in arrears	£12,228
A Level Pension payable for your life monthly in advance	£11,441
A Level Pension payable for your life monthly in advance and guaranteed for a period of five years	£11,234
A Pension payable for your life paid monthly in advance for a minimum period of five years and escalating at 5% p.a.	£7,694
A Pension payable for your life + spouse's pension	£10,019
A Pension payable for your life + spouse's pension both escalating at 5% p.a.	£6,403

BUDGET CHANGES 1994

How much pension income you will actually receive from your pension fund on retirement depends to a large extent on the Annuity Rates available to you at the date of your retirement. Pension Annuity Rates are closely linked to long term Interest Rates. Long term Interest Rates have fallen significantly over recent years, and so have pension annuity rates. This fall in annuity rates has had dire consequences for many pensioners.

In the November 1994 Budget the Chancellor announced the introduction of flexible pension annuities from May 1995. So, if at your chosen retirement date annuity rates are low you can extend your pension investment period up to your 75th Birthday and you can draw down annual income from your pension fund without committing yourself finally to a low lifetime annuity rate.

OPEN MARKET OPTION Many pension providers now provide what is called the Open Market Option. This facilitates you in purchasing the best pension for yourself at retirement and it works like this: once you decide to retire, you may take your accumulated retirement fund and place it with whichever authorised Life Assurance Company you consider is offering you the best pension terms in your individual circumstances at that time. It may be the company with which you have accumulated the fund or it may not. It is up to you to decide which Life Assurance Company is best for you.

Comment: Check if your pension plan has this Open Market Option.

Tax Relief

The percentage of your net relevant earnings qualifying for tax relief depends on your age and plan type.

Plan Type

Your type of plan is decided by when you commenced contributions. If you commenced before the 1st July 1988 it is the *old-type* plan. If you commenced after the 1st July 1988 it is a *new-type* plan.

The following percentages of net relevant earnings qualify for tax relief under each plan type as follows:

Age on 6th April	Old-Type Plan	New-Type Plan
up to 35	17.5	17.5
36 to 45	17.5	20.0
46 to 50	17.5	25.0
51 to 55	20.0	30.0
56 to 60	22.5	35.0
61 to 74	27.5	40.0
Over 74	NIL	NIL

Your employer may also contribute towards the new type of personal pension plan within the above limits. If however you are using a personal pension plan to contract-out of SERPS, the SERPS amounts do not count towards contribution limits outlined above.

Net Relevant Earnings

If you are an employee, your net relevant earnings are, in general terms, your gross earnings, plus taxable fringe benefits, less allowable expenses. If you are self-employed, your net relevant earnings will normally mean taxable profits, less capital allowances, stock relief and any losses from earlier years which have not been offset against other income.

In the 1989/90 tax year a cap of £60,000 was placed on net relevant earnings qualifying for tax relief on personal pension plans. This earnings cap will be increased each year in line with the Retail Price Index. For the 1995/96 tax year the capped figure is £78,600. No income limit is applicable on the old-type plans.

Maximum Contributions

The rules are complicated and depend to some extent on how much you have paid in previous years.

Carry-Back Rules

The carry-back rules allow you to claim tax relief in a previous year, provided the premium was paid in the current tax year and you have enough unused tax-relief in that year to cover the amount carried back. If you had no net relevant earnings in the previous year, you can carry-back the contribution two years and get tax relief at your highest rate applicable in that year.

Carry-Forward Rules

If you have not made the maximum pension contributions over the past six years, you may now make additional contributions to take advantage of these unused reliefs by way of what are called the "carry-forward rules".

Example: Eric's position is as follows:

Tax Year	Net Relevant Earnings	Maximum Contribution Entitlements	Contributions Paid Already	Possible Additional Contributions
1994/95	£35,000	£6,125	£1,000	£5,125
1993/94	£33,000	£5,775	£1,000	£4,775
1992/93	£27,000	£4,725	£1,000	£3,725
1991/92	£29,000	£5,075	£1,000	£4,075
1990/91	£21,000	£3,675	£1,000	£2,675
1989/90	£13,000	£2,275	£1,000	£1,275
1988/89	£11,000	£1,925	-	£1,925
Total				£23,575
Deduct Current Year's Possible Additional Contribution -				£4,775
Relief Available for Back Years -				£18,800

89

Eric now wishes to pay, say £12,000, in addition to his regular annual pension contribution of £1,000, under the carry forward rules.

He must pay the maximum contributions in the current year before the carry-forward rules operate. The total allowable contribution for the current year is £6,125 (17.5% of £35,000) of which he has already paid £1,000. So, £6,875 (i.e. £12,000 less £5,125) is available to be offset against previous years' unused reliefs.

Eric's new tax reliefs will work out as follows:

1988/89	£1,925
1989/90	£1,275
1990/91	£2,675
1991/92	£1,000
Total	£6,875

This additional tax allowance of £6,875 will be offset against Eric's current year's taxable income. So, the additional contributions under carry-forward rules will not affect his actual tax position in previous years.

Normally, you cannot continue to contribute to a personal pension plan after benefits have commenced. So, any unused relief should be used up before retirement.

CLAIMING TAX-RELIEF

Employees

Employees initially get basic rate relief on contributions paid to an approved personal pension at source. If you are a higher-rate tax payer, you may claim the higher relief on form PP120. Your tax inspector can arrange extra relief through your PAYE code or by rebate at the end of the tax year.

Self-Employed

If you are self-employed you will not get tax relief at source. Include the deduction on your tax return or complete form PP120 to claim the refund or ask your tax inspector to adjust your final tax assessment for the year in question.

If you do pay excess contributions into an *old-type* plan, you will not get tax relief on the excess. If you pay excess contributions into a *new-type* plan the excess contributions will be refunded.

PERSONAL PENSION PLANS vs

EMPLOYEE PENSION PLANS

The Inland Revenue allow the self-employed and people in non-pensionable employment to contribute a fixed percentage of their net relevant earnings to a personal pension plan with full tax-relief. Up to 5% of net relevant earnings within these same limits may be used to purchase life assurance cover.

Employers, on the other hand, may contribute whatever contributions are necessary to build up a pension fund, which will provide their employees with a pension of 2/3rds final pensionable salary, plus a widow's and dependent's pension, plus the annual escalation in the value of these pensions to offset the increases in the cost of living during retirement.

To illustrate this point, let us take a look at Eric in non-pensionable employment wishing to retire at age 65, embarking on a personal plan now. The maximum percentage of his net relevant earnings which he may contribute to a personal pension plan with full tax relief are as follows:

Age on 6th April	Maximum Pension Contribution as % of Net Relevant Earnings
up to 35	17.5%
36 to 45	20.0%
46 to 50	25.0%
51 to 55	30.0%
56 to 60	35.0%
61 to 74	40.0%

Let us assume that Eric now starts making these maximum annual contributions to a personal pension plan. The chart below illustrates his *average* yearly contributions as a percentage of his net relevant earnings, between the date of commencement and retirement age.

Eric's Age when he Commenced the Plan	Eric's Average Annual Contribution as % of his Net Relevant Earnings
30	26.14%
40	29.20%
50	34.00%
60	39.00%

However, if Eric was an employee, Eric's employer could make the pension contributions illustrated below and get full tax relief on these payments, assuming Eric had no existing pension provision and that he will have 20 years' service with his employer at retirement age. It is also assumed that all the assumptions in the illustration on page 78 are applicable.

Pension contributions below are shown as a percentage of Eric's pensionable salary and it is assumed that they commenced at one of the relevant ages.

Eric's Age when Contributions Commenced	Maximum Annual Contributions as % of Eric's Salary
30	106%
40	120%
50	148%
60	263%

If Eric's employer fails to provide the maximum pension benefits allowed, he (Eric) may normally contribute up to 15% of his salary by way of AVC or FSAVC to boost his existing pension benefits and claim tax relief on these contributions.

Women fare even better within employer's pension schemes, as they tend to live longer and retire earlier than men. They thus require a larger pension fund at normal retirement age to provide maximum pension benefits.

If you are self-employed or in non-pensionable employment, you should start making personal contributions as early as possible, preferably in your early twenties.

If you have not already made the necessary pension contributions to provide yourself with adequate pension income in retirement, you could consider becoming an "employee", for example by operating your business under a limited liability company with the aim of building up at least 20 years' service before retirement. Your "employer" could then provide your pension benefits in a tax-efficient manner.

Conclusion

As an employee or self-employed person, how well you do in the pension stakes is, to a surprisingly large extent, up to you .

Part Two of this Guide has provided you with the basic guidelines for planning your future pension benefits and financial security. More information of particular relevance to your own situation will always be beneficial. So, our concluding advice is to arm yourself with as much information as you can amass on this subject. If you are still unsure, contact a Pension Adviser and start planning your financial future **NOW**. After a lifetime of hard work the very last thing you need in retirement is a financial headache.

"You can't just go on being a good egg. You must either hatch or go back."

C.S. Lewis

PART THREE

THE TAX SYSTEM

THE PAYE SYSTEM

FOREIGN EMPLOYMENT

CAPITAL GAINS TAX

INHERITANCE TAX

MAKING A WILL

THE TAX SYSTEM

THE INLAND REVENUE

Day to day control of the tax system is exercised by the Board of the Inland Revenue, who have the responsibility for levying and collecting direct taxes. The UK is divided into many tax districts, to which District Tax Inspectors are appointed. Under a District Inspector a team of specialist Inspectors operate in two broad areas - Employed taxpayers and Self-Employed taxpayers. Tax Inspectors have responsibility for agreeing individual tax liabilities and issuing tax assessments.

If you disagree with your Tax Inspector's computation of your tax liability, you can appeal against it, whether or not you have received an assessment.

Taxes agreed between individuals and their Tax Inspector are collected by the Collector of Taxes; similarly, tax due on a notice of assessment is collected by the Collector unless appealed and a request is made for a postponement of payment.

In this section of the book, we outline three major areas of personal tax:

- **INCOME TAX**
- **CAPITAL GAINS TAX**
- **INHERITANCE TAX**

INCOME TAX

ANNUAL RETURNS Taxpayers are obliged to submit a tax return within thirty days of being requested to do so. The revenue will normally allow more time if required. However, if the return is not submitted before the 31st October you may become liable to interest on any tax due. Tax return forms for 1995/96 will be sent out to taxpayers from April 1995 onwards. These cover income and outgoings for the year ended 5th April 1995 and personal allowances and an estimate of tax-deductible expenses for the year ended 5th April 1996.

In theory, your Tax Inspector can ask you to submit a tax return every year. However, if your tax affairs are comparatively straightforward, you may only be required to file returns approximately every three years, or even less frequently.

Remember, it is an offence to deliberately give false information on your tax return, so check it thoroughly before you sign it.

ASSESSMENTS In general, assessments will not be raised until after your tax return has been submitted and the assessment will be based on the information included on your return. If you default in making a return, or if your Inspector is dissatisfied with your return, an estimated assessment may be raised as to the amount of tax due by you.

APPEALS An appeal against a Notice of Assessment must be made in writing within thirty days of the date of issue. Outside of this thirty day deadline, an appeal will be admitted only if you can successfully show that there was good reason for the delay.

Even if you are appealing against it, unless you ask for a postponement of payment, the tax due on a Notice of Assessment must be paid. Your Tax Inspector will generally agree only to postpone payment of the amount of tax in dispute. When the appeal is settled, a revised assessment will be issued and the additional tax due, if any, must be paid within thirty days of the date of the revised assessment or the date on which the original tax was due, if later.

SELF ASSESSMENT

Self Assessment is a major change to the tax system which will simplify tax rules for people who are obliged to complete tax returns.

You are normally obliged to complete a tax return annually if you are self employed, a business partner, a company director, an employee who pays tax at the higher rate or an employee or pensioner with complex tax affairs.

These changes will not come into effect until the 1996/97 tax year.

The new Self Assessment rules will strictly define when tax returns have to be completed and when tax has to be paid. There will be automatic penalties for missing deadlines, so it is in your own best interest to make sure that you keep your tax affairs fully up to date.

If you are not obliged to fill in a tax return self assessment will not really affect you as PAYE and other arrangements for deducting tax at source will continue as they do now.

CLASSIFICATION OF INCOME

Income is classified under a number of headings. These headings are known as schedules and the income falling under each schedule is as follows:

Schedule A:

Rental Income from land or property. Excluded, is income from furnished lettings which is taxed under Schedule D Case I or Case VI.

Schedule C:

Interest from British Government Loans and National Savings Banks.

Schedule D:

Case I:	Profits from trade
Case II:	Profits froma profession
Case III:	Interest from loans, annuities and other regular annual payments.
Case IV and V	All foreign income.
Case VI:	Income from occasional miscellaneous sources, plus rental income from furnished lettings.

NOTE: From 6th April 1995 all rental income from property situated in the UK will be taxed under Schedule A.

Schedule E:

Income from offices or employment, together with pensions, benefits-in-kind, and certain lump sum payments arising from your office or employment.

Case I	Earnings received by UK Residents and ordinary residents.
Case II	Earnings received by individuals who are resident but not ordinary resident in the UK.
Case III	Earnings on work carried out abroad.

Schedule F:

Dividends and unit trust distributions.

COMPUTATION OF AN INDIVIDUAL'S INCOME-TAX LIABILITY

Income tax is payable on your taxable income. Your taxable income is your total income assessable for tax, less deductions for personal allowances and outgoings which may be offset against your taxable income.

TAX ALLOWANCES

		1993/94 £	1994/95 £	1995/96 £
Personal Allowance	- Under 65	3,445	3,445	3,525
	- 65 to 74	4,200	4,200	4,630
	- 75 and over	4,370	4,370	4,800
Married Couple's Allowance	- Under 65	1,720	1,720	*1,720
	- 65 to 74	2,465	2,665	*2,995
	- 75 and over	2,505	2,705	*3,035
Income Limit for Age-Related Allowances		14,200	14,200	14,600
Additional Personal Allowance for Children		1,720	1,720	*1,720
Widow's Bereavement Allowance		1,720	1,720	*1,720
Blind Person's Allowance		1,080	1,200	1,200

* From 6th April 1994 the married couples allowance including the higher allowances for the over 65's, the widow's bereavement allowance and the additional personal allowance is given at the 20% rate only, and from 6th April 1995 these allowances will be given at 15%.

AGE ALLOWANCE If your income exceeds £14,600 in the current year (1995/96), the age allowance is reduced by £1 for each £2 by which your income is above the income limit, until it reaches the level of the ordinary single person's or married man's allowance.

BLIND PERSON'S ALLOWANCE Any person registered as blind with a local authority can claim this allowance.

OTHER TAX ALLOWANCES

In addition to the above allowances, further tax relief may be claimed for the following:

- Premiums paid for life assurance on policies taken out before 14th March 1984. The relief is 12.5 per cent for 1995/96, up to a maximum of £1,500 or one sixth of your total income, whichever is the higher.

- Premiums paid for private medical insurance, provided you or your spouse are over 60. You can also get relief on premiums paid on behalf of someone else, provided that person is also over 60 years of age. From 6th April 1994 relief is restricted to the basic rate (25%).

- Premiums paid into approved retirement annuity schemes or personal pension plans.
- Interest paid on loans up to £30,000 to buy your sole or main residence or if the loans were taken out on or before 5th April 1988 to improve it. From 6th April 1994 mortgage interest relief is given at 20% and from 6th April 1995 it is given at 15%.
- Payments made to registered charities under a deed of covenant and existing covenants to individuals on which you are already getting tax relief. Covenants to individuals taken out after the 14th March 1988 do not qualify for tax relief. You can also get tax relief on payments made to charities under an employer's approved payroll-giving scheme or through Gift Aid.
- From 1992/93 and subsequent tax years tax relief is available on fees paid for courses leading to a national vocational qualification, if you contribute towards your own training.
- The Enterprise Investment Scheme (EIS) was introduced in 1993. If you invest in a qualifying EIS, tax relief at 20% is available up to an annual limit of £100,000 provided you keep the shares for at least 5 years. Relief is given in the year which you subscribe for EIS.
- From 6th April 1995 you can invest in a Venture Capital Trust and claim tax relief at 20% on your investment. The maximum investment in a tax year is £100,00 and the shares must be held for at least 5 years.

THE TAX BANDS 1995/96

Taxable Income	Tax Rate	Cumulative Tax
0 - £3,200	20%	£640
£3,201 - £24,300	25%	£5,915
Over £24,300	40%	

THE TAX BANDS 1994/95

Taxable Income	Tax Rate	Cumulative Tax
0 - £3,000	20%	£600
£3,001 - £23,700	25%	£5,775
Over £23,700	40%	

THE PAYE SYSTEM

If you have income from employments or pensions you are normally taxed under PAYE (Pay As You Earn).

The system ensures that the excess of your weekly or monthly pay over your personal allowances and outgoings is taxed on a regular basis.

TAXABLE EARNINGS For our purposes here taxable earnings are your gross pay, less superannuation contributions and the Tax-Free Allowances on your Notice of Coding.

NOTICE OF CODING You may receive a notice of coding in January or February preceding the relevant tax year or when you claim a new allowance or inform your tax inspector of a new source of income. Your notice of coding sets out the amount of allowances and outgoings to be set against your earnings in the current tax year and is the amount which you can earn tax free. When you receive your notice of coding check it carefully for:

Allowances
Expenses
Deductions
Tax Code (Prefix and Suffix Letters)

You can check the first three in the relevant sections in Part Four of this Guide.

To enable your employer operate the PAYE System he/she will need to know:

- Your Tax Code.
- Your Tax Letter.

TAX CODE Your code is made up of numbers and a letter. The number tells your employer the amount of pay you may get free of tax: for example, if your tax code is 278L, your tax-free allowances are £2,789 per annum. The letters generally segregate taxpayers into categories, the following being the most usual:

L If you are under 65 years of age and single.

H If you or your spouse are under 65 years of age claiming the married couple's allowance for those under 65, or the additional personal allowance.

P If you are aged 65 to 74.

V If you or your spouse are aged 65 to 74 and claiming the married couple's allowance for those aged 65 to 74.

If your tax code includes the letters L, H P or V, your employer may change your tax-free allowance to comply with budget changes.

T	T is given under certain circumstances - e.g. if you get a reduced amount of age-related allowance, if you get the age-related personal allowance for people who turn 75 or more during the tax year, if you have a company car, or if you do not want your employer to know your age or marital status.
F	These codes are normally used if you have a second job. All of your pay will be taxed at either the basic or the higher rate, because all your tax allowances will be used against the income you receive from your main employment.
K	From 6th April 1993 a new system of K codes commenced. This new code is for employees, who receive employment perks the value of which exceed their personal tax allowances. If you are on a K code your employer will add the benefit amount to your taxable pay.

There are also three codes which do not have numbers, or if they have numbers they are not part of your tax-free allowance and they tell your employer what rate of tax is applicable to your total pay:

BR Your pay is to be taxed at the basic rate only.

D (followed by a number) - your pay is to be taxed at the higher rate of tax

NT No tax is payable on your income.

TAX TABLES

Your employer has a number of tax tables, which are to be used as appropriate.

Table A:	Table A shows the total tax-free pay you are entitled to on any one pay day.
Table B:	Table B shows the tax due on your taxable pay at the basic rate.
Table C:	Table C shows the tax due on your taxable pay at the higher rate.
Table D:	Table D coding is normally used for taxing employment income other than your main employment income.
Table F:	These are ready reckoners that apply only to employees who have tax codes that begin with the letter F.

The tax code is operated on a cumulative basis to calculate how much tax is deductible or refundable on a particular pay date. Your employer does this by comparing your total tax liability to date with the tax you have already paid.

If the tax you have already paid to date is greater than your tax liability on any pay day, you will get a tax refund and if it is less, you pay more.

STUDENT EMPLOYMENT INCOME

Students may be liable to pay tax on earnings from vacation jobs. As a UK student, you may complete Form P38S if your total earnings, together with any other taxable income you may have, is less than your personal allowances. This will exempt your employer from deducting tax under PAYE from your vacation earnings. Remember, housing benefit, student grants, scholarships and most research rewards are exempt from income tax.

PAYE EMERGENCY TAX

The emergency code is a special code employers use when a relevant tax code has not been received from you. This can happen for example, if you had not produced a notice of tax coding or a form P45 when you commenced employment. Your employer will operate the emergency code on a weekly or monthly basis until your tax status is sorted out.

When you are taxed on the emergency basis, you are entitled only to a single person's allowance. If you are entitled to a higher allowance, the emergency code will mean you are paying too much tax. You will get a refund when you are allocated a proper tax code.

PAYE REFUNDS

PAYE operates under a cumulative system for pay and tax-free allowances in each tax year. If on any pay day your cumulative code exceeds your cumulative taxable pay, your employer will not deduct any tax. He may even refund some or all of the tax already paid since the preceding 6th of April.

Example: Your gross pay is £250 per week and your tax code is 364L, your position in Week 30 is as follows:

Position at	Cumulative Pay	Cumulative Tax Code	Cumulative Taxable Pay	Cumulative Tax
	£	£	£	£
Week 30	7,500	2,105	5,395	1,349

Following a claim for extra allowances etc, your Tax Inspector issued, in Week 31, a new Notice of Coding showing 484L. Your position in Week 31 is as follows:

Position at	Cumulative Pay	Cumulative Tax Code	Cumulative Taxable Pay	Cumulative Tax
	£	£	£	£
Week 31	7,750	2,891	4,859	1,215

Since £1,349 has already been paid, you will be due a tax refund of £134.

NOTE: Where the Week 1 / Month 1 or emergency basis applies, no
refund of tax may be made by the employer, as cumulative
tax-free allowances or cumulative pay are not taken into account.
Similarly refunds may not be made if you have prefix codes D, F
or NT.

REFUND WHERE THE EMPLOYEE IS ABSENT DUE TO ILLNESS If you
are absent from work due to illness and you continue to be paid, deductions or
refunds of tax will continue to be made in the normal way. If you are not
entitled to receive any pay your normal pay day and the cumulative basis
applies, you will be entitled to a refund of tax, in accordance with the
cumulative tax-free allowance applying on that day.

Example:

Your pay is £300 per week and your tax-free pay is £84 per week applied
cumulatively and your tax rate is 25%. Your illness commences in Week 13 and
you receive no pay. Your refund for Week 13 will work out as follows:

Position at	Cumulative Tax	Cumulative Tax Code	Cumulative Taxable Pay	Cumulative Tax
	£	£	£	£
Week 12	3,600	1,008	2,592	648
Week 13	3,600	1,092	2,508	627
			Refund	21

**ABSENT FROM WORK FOR SOME CAUSE OTHER THAN ILLNESS, e.g.
STRIKE.** Normally, your employer will not make tax refunds if you are absent
from work because of a trade dispute. There are, however, exemptions to this
rule: if you leave that employment during the strike, or if your employer is
authorised by the Tax Office to make the refund. Refunds will normally be
made when you go back to work.

REFUND DURING UNEMPLOYMENT

If you claim Unemployment Benefit, any refunds due to you after you leave
work will normally be made by the Benefit Office, after you start work again, or
after you submit a tax return at the end of the tax year. However, if you become
unemployed and do not claim Unemployment Benefit, you may claim a refund
on Form P50 from your Tax Office after about four weeks of unemployment.

PAYE REFUND AFTER THE YEAR-END The tax year ends on 5th April and sometime after this date your employer will give you a form P60. This P60 is an important document as it is an official statement of your gross pay, tax and national insurance contributions paid in a relevant year. You have a legal right to this document.

If there are any additional allowances or deductions which you have not claimed in the past six tax years, these should now be documented and forwarded with your relevant P60 to your Inspector of Taxes, requesting a tax refund.

TAX UNDERPAYMENTS As stated earlier PAYE operates on a cumulative basis so if your tax code is reduced during the tax year you will find yourself paying considerable more tax on a particular payday.

Example:

Your gross pay is £350 per week and your tax code up to week 10 was 328L. In week 11 your tax code was reduced to 278L. Your position in week 10, 11 and 12 could be illustrated as follows, assuming you pay tax at 25%.

Position at	Cummulative Pay	Cummulative Code	Cummulative Taxable Pay	Cummulative Tax
Week 10	£3,500	£632	£2,868	£717
Week 11	£3,850	£590	£3,260	£815
Week 12	£4,200	£644	£3,556	£889

In these circumstances your average weekly tax payment would have been £71.70 up to week 10. Your actual tax payment in week 11 would have been £98 and £74 in week 12 and subsequent weeks.

PAYE UNDERPAYMENT AFTER THE YEAR END If your tax code was incorrect during previous tax years or if you had a taxable source of income not taxed, tax arrears may be collected by your inspector by way of a cash lump sum payment or by instalments through the PAYE system.

If the back tax is a significantly large amount or applicable to income outside the PAYE system your inspector will probably demand a lump sum payment plus interest from the date the tax was originally due. The rate of interest applicable to income tax arrears at date of publication was 5.5% per annum. Interest charges of less than £30.00 are generally ignored.

PAYING BY INSTALMENTS If you are an employee or a pensioner and the amount of your back tax is not a significantly large amount your inspector may collect these arrears by way of a reduction in your PAYE code over a number of years. Arrears paid through the PAYE system are not normally subject to interest charges.

Official Errors

If your tax is in arrears due to "Official Errors" these arrears may not be payable or only partly payable if:

- You have provided your inspector with your full tax detail correctly and on time.
- You have taken reasonable care to keep your tax affairs in order and up to date.
- It was reasonable for you to assume that no extra tax was due and
- Your inspector did not inform you of your tax arrears until after the end of the tax year following that one in which the tax was actually due.

If all these conditions are met and provided your income falls within the gross income limits applicable to tax remission. The schedule below outlines the fraction of tax arrears payable after 1st February 1993.

Tax Remission Limits after 1st February 1993

Income Limit	Fraction of tax arrears collected
up to £15,500	None
£15,501 - £18,000	1/4
£18,001 - £22,000	1/2
£22,001 - £26,000	3/4
£26,001 - £40,000	9/10
above £40,000	All

FOREIGN EMPLOYMENT

EMPLOYMENT OUTSIDE THE UK

GENERAL PRINCIPLES The extent of your liability to income tax in the UK depends on whether you are:

- resident in the UK
- ordinarily resident in the UK
- domiciled in the UK

RESIDENCE You are deemed to be resident in the UK for tax-purposes, if any of the following apply:

- You spend more than 183 days here in a tax year (ignoring the days of arrival and departure).
- You visit the UK year after year and these visits exceed 90 days per year on average over 4 consecutive years.
- You are a British or Irish subject, ordinarily resident in the UK and occasionally resident abroad.
- Up to the 5th April 1993 you would have been regarded as resident in the UK if you had a place of abode available for your own use in the UK (e.g. a house or flat) and you visited here in the tax year.

ORDINARY RESIDENCE A person is said to be ordinarily resident in the country in which he/she lives on a permanent basis.

RESIDENCE v ORDINARY RESIDENCE Let us suppose that you have lived in the UK all your life and leave the country for a full tax year (i.e. from 6th April to the following 5th April) with the intention of returning to the UK after your temporary absence abroad. You will not be regarded as resident in the UK for tax purposes in that tax year but you will be regarded as ordinarily resident for that tax year.

DOMICILE You can only have one domicile and this is generally taken to be the country which you regard as your natural home e.g. country of birth.

RESIDENT BUT NOT DOMICILED IN THE UK If you are resident but not domiciled in the UK (e.g. a citizen of the United States working in London for a temporary period of five years), you will be liable to UK income tax in full on your UK income. Foreign income will be liable only to the extent that it is remitted into the UK.

DOUBLE TAXATION Generally, a UK resident is liable to UK income tax on worldwide income and non-UK residents are liable to UK income tax on income arising in the UK. As similar provisions apply in other countries, this may give rise to double taxation, so the purpose of double taxation agreements is to prevent this by:

- exempting certain income from tax in one country or
- by offsetting the tax paid on the income in one country against the tax liability on that same income in another country.

WORKING ABROAD

How your foreign employment income will be taxed in the UK is normally determined by:

- Residence Status
- Length of your stay(s) abroad.
- Domicile.

SHORT-TERM EMPLOYMENT:

If you are resident and ordinarily resident in the UK and you go abroad for short periods to work, your foreign income may be subject to UK tax. Expenses and taxable benefits paid outside the UK may also be subject to UK tax, assuming you are a higher paid employee.

However, if you perform your UK and overseas duties under similar contracts, the costs of travelling to and between foreign destinations may be tax-deductible, if this travel is deemed to be in the course of performing your duties. Similarly subsistence expenses incurred on overseas trips could be tax-deductible. The costs of medical insurance and medical treatment incurred while abroad on overseas assignments are specifically exempt from tax.

Example:
Eric spends 3 months working in France, he earns the equivalent of £6,000 in 1994/95 and paid £2,000 in tax. His UK income for 1994/95 was £2,000.

		1994/95
French Income		£6,000
UK Income		£2,000
		£8,000
Personal Allowance		£3,445
		£4,555
Tax £3,000 @ 20%	£600	
£1,555 @ 25%	£389	
	£989	
Credit for French Tax	£2,000	
UK Income Tax Payable	Nil	

Foreign Tax Paid

Generally, any foreign tax paid may be credited against your UK income tax liability on that same income in the UK. If your effective rate of foreign tax is higher than the corresponding UK rate, the excess foreign tax is an additional cost to you. Some relief from this foreign tax may be available, where the Inland Revenue have negotiated a comprehensive double taxation agreement between the UK and the country concerned.

FOREIGN ASSIGNMENTS:

Under longer-term foreign assignments, you can claim 100% relief from UK tax on earnings, even if you remain resident in the UK for tax purposes. This applies only if all or part of your employment duties were performed outside the UK and you were abroad for a substantial period(s) of time.

To claim this relief, you must have been working abroad for 365 days or more within a qualifying period.

You may be abroad for the whole of the qualifying period or, alternatively, you can return to the UK for short visits, provided no intervening period in the UK is longer than sixty-two days and the total number of days in the UK is not more than one-sixth of the total number of days in the qualifying period.

So, you can have a succession of periods in the UK and abroad and still qualify for the 100% deduction.

Example:

Charles was on a foreign assignment for his employer from the 3rd September 1993 to the 22nd February 1995. His trips to the UK and the number of days working abroad were as follows:

Location	Dates	No. of Days
Abroad	From 03.09.93 to 11.12.93	100
UK	From 12.12.93 to 19.02.94	70
Abroad	From 20.02.94 to 07.07.94	140
UK	From 08.07.94 to 05.09.94	60
Abroad	From 06.09.94 to 22.02.95	170

The first trip to the UK breaks the 62 day rule, so his first 100 days abroad are excluded. The new qualifying period starts again from the 20th February 1994. At the end of the third trip abroad, he has spent 60 days in the UK out of a total of 370.

This is a qualifying period, as his stay in the UK from the 8th July 1994 to the 5th September 1994 is less than 62 days and also less than 1/6th of the total qualifying period.

So Charles' earnings abroad over this period qualify for 100% UK tax reduction.

LONG-TERM EMPLOYMENT ABROAD:

If you are non-resident here for tax purposes, you are liable only to UK tax on certain income arising in the UK. So, if you take up long-term employment abroad and you can demonstrate that you have relinquished your UK tax-resident status here, you should complete Form P85. The Inland Revenue may grant you a provisional non-resident ruling effective from the date following your departure. Non-resident status is normally granted if:

- all your employment duties are performed abroad
- your employment and your absence from the UK will extend over a complete tax year
- your interim visits during the period will not amount to more than six months in any one year or average not more than three months per tax year.

This provisional ruling is usually confirmed after one complete tax year abroad. If evidence of non-residence is not available, you may not be given provisional non-resident status for three years and during this three-year period you may continue to be taxed provisionally as a UK resident.

Income Exempted from UK Tax

When you can satisfy the Inland Revenue that you are leaving the UK and that you will be non-resident here for tax purposes for the remainder of that tax year, they will review your income tax file and ignore any earnings you may expect in the country of your destination. This will in effect give you a full year's tax-free allowance in the year of your departure to offset against your UK income in that tax year.

Example:

Eric is single and worked in the UK from the 6th April to the 31st July 1994, when he emigrated to the USA.

Eric's UK income for the tax year 1994/95 was £7,000 and he paid £1,475 tax.

Eric's tax position as a non-resident is as follows:

	1994/95	
Salary	£7,000	
Personal Allowances	£3,445	
	£3,555	
Tax £3,000 @ 20%		£600
Tax £555 @ 25%		£139
		£739
Tax Paid		£1,475
Tax Refund Due		£736

IMMIGRANTS STARTING EMPLOYMENT IN THE UK

When you commence work in the UK you will be asked to complete a Residence Enquiry Form P86 and a Tax Coding Form P15. How you will be taxed on your employment income in the UK is partly determined by whether or not you are categorised as a 'qualifying non-resident', the length of time you decide to stay in the UK this year and over the next four years, or if you have accommodation available here.

If it is your intention to work and take up short term residence in the UK, your UK employment income will normally be taxed under PAYE on a 'week one' basis. However, if it is your intention to work and take up long-term residence in the UK, you may be taxed on PAYE cumulative basis i.e. the UK tax authorities will issue you with a tax-free allowance from the 6th April preceding your arrival in the UK. A new permanent resident in the UK is entitled to a full personal allowance. However, non-residents are not normally entitled to these allowances unless they fall into the 'qualifying non-residence' category.

'Qualifying non-resident' status includes the following:

- A citizen of the UK, the commonwealth or of the Republic of Ireland
- A person who is or has been in the service of the Crown
- A person employed in the service of any missionary society
- A person employed in the service of any territory under Her Majesty's protection
- A resident of the Channel Islands or the Isle of Man
- A former UK resident who is resident abroad for health reasons.
- A widow whose late husband was in Crown service

- A resident and/or national of a country with which the UK has a double tax treaty providing specifically for this relief, for example:

  Austria, Mauritius, Belgium, Namibia, Netherlands, Fiji, Norway, Finland, Singapore, Greece, Swaziland, Indonesia, Switzerland, Germany, Israel, Zambia, Luxembourg.

After the 6th April 1990, as a 'qualifying non-resident' you are entitled to claim full personal allowances as a UK resident. So, your new position for the above example would be as follows in the 1994/95 tax year:

	1994/95
UK Earnings	£5,000
Personal Allowance	£3,445
Taxable Income	£1,555
Tax £1,555 @ 20%	£311
Tax Paid	£1,200
Tax Refund Due	£889

If you are taxed on a week one/month one basis, under PAYE you receive the benefit of only part of your personal allowance. You are however, entitled to offset full personal allowances against your UK employment income, so you could be entitled to a tax refund on your return home.

In order to get this refund from the UK tax authorities, complete a Form P85 and send it with your Form P45 at the end of the relevant tax year to your tax inspector at the address shown on your notice of coding.

LONG-TERM EMPLOYMENT IN THE UK

If you spend less than 183 days in the UK during a tax year, you will normally be regarded as being non-resident. If you visit the UK for an average of more than 90 days each tax year for four consecutive years, you will be regarded as becoming resident and ordinarily resident here.

If your assignment in the UK is going to be for more than two years but less than three, you will be treated as being resident but not ordinarily resident from the date of your arrival. If your assignment exceeds three years, you will be regarded as becoming ordinarily resident here.

When you arrive in the UK, you will complete Form P86 and P15 and the Inland Revenue will grant you a provisional ruling regarding your residence status here. If you are granted full residence status, you may claim full personal allowances in the year of arrival, and any foreign earnings you may have had before you arrived in the UK will be ignored.

112

Example:

George came from the USA to live permanently in London in July 1994, when he was granted full residence status. His US income before departure was £7,000, his UK income for 1994/95 was £15,000.

George's tax position as a permanent resident will be as follows:

		1994/95
UK Income		£15,000
Personal Allowances		£3,445
Taxable		£11,555
£3,000 @ 20%	£600	
£8,555 @ 25%	£2,139	£2,739
UK Tax Payable		£2,739

REMITTANCE BASIS

If you are not domiciled in the UK but are resident and ordinarily resident here and work for an overseas employer wholly outside the UK and the Republic of Ireland, tax on a remittance basis may apply to earnings from that employment. This is so, provided that no part of your duties, other than incidental duties relating to this overseas employment, are performed in the UK and that the remuneration attributed to your overseas employment is at a rate appropriate to the duties of that employment and without regard to your UK employment duties.

If you are resident in the UK but are neither domiciled nor ordinarily resident here and you perform duties for an overseas employer both here and abroad, your remuneration for duties performed in the UK are taxable in full and your remuneration for duties performed abroad will be taxed on a remittance basis.

The apportionment between your UK remuneration and your overseas remuneration is normally a question of fact. However, where no separate contract of employment exists for each employment the Inland Revenue may accept an apportionment of your total remuneration based on the number of days worked in the UK and the number of days worked abroad.

OTHER INCOME

TAX INSPECT

Example:

George is not domiciled or ordinarily resident here for tax purposes, in the 1994/95 tax year. His total earnings were £50,000. He spent 110 out of his 220 working days in Saudi Arabia. George's income assessable to UK tax on a remittance basis may be calculated as follows:

$$\frac{110}{220} \quad \text{x} \quad £50,000 = £25,000$$

If the amount paid to George in the UK, including benefits and remittances, is not more than £25,000, he will be taxed on £25,000. If the amount received in the UK exceeds £25,000, he will be taxed on that higher amount.

Remittance basis may also apply to the following income, if you are resident but not domiciled in the UK:

- Investment income from a non-UK source.
- Income from trades which are managed and controlled overseas.

Remittance can be made in cash or in kind. For example, if you bought a car abroad out of your overseas income and brought it back into the UK, this may be treated as a remittance for tax purposes.

DOMICILE

Your domicile is normally the country you regard as your natural home. However, you may be in a position to choose a domicile if you have terminated all links with your domicile of origin and have established permanent roots in a new country. Foreign income received by non-domiciled UK residents receive more favourable tax treatment than does foreign income received by UK domiciled residents. So you should consider the following points carefully before you decide to change your domicile.

If you have a continuous source of income outside the UK, which you had been remitting before you became resident here, try and avoid any remittance in the year before you officially become resident, otherwise this income may be taxed.

If you cannot stop your foreign income remittances and you also have capital funds abroad, isolate your capital funds in a separate bank account and make your remittances from this capital account, as far as possible. This may reduce your exposure to UK tax. Remember if you remit funds out of an account containing both capital and income, the Inland Revenue may regard that remittance as income up to the level of income appropriate to that account. Also, if you are not domiciled in the UK, any remittance made in the year after your source of foreign income has ceased is not chargable to UK tax.

TAX-FREE BENEFITS/EXPENSES

Normally benefits and expenses are tax-free only if allowed by *statute* or if incurred "wholly, exclusively and necessarily in the performance of the duties of your employment". Some expenses are, tax-free *by concession*:

- **Meal Vouchers,** provided they are non-transferable and the value does not exceed 15p for each working day.

- **Travelling Expenses** between various locations during the course of employment. Travelling expenses from home to your place of employment are taxable as are round-sum allowances to cover all expenses you may incur in the performance of your duties.

- **Travelling and Subsistence** expenses incurred on behalf of employees during public transport strikes or industrial action.

- **Travelling Expenses** between home and work incurred by employers on behalf of severely and permanently disabled persons who are because of their disability incapable of using public transport.

- **Further Education or Training**: If you have to travel from your normal place of work to attend a course, additional expenses incurred in travelling to and from the course and reasonable subsistence payments are payable tax-free (maximum £7,000 p.a.).

- **Long-Service Award:** If the period of service is not less than 20 years and no previous awards have been made to the recipient within the previous ten years, provided the cost to the employer does not exceed £20 for each year of service.

- **Suggestion Scheme Awards** If the amount of the award does not exceed 50% of the expected net financial benefit during the first year of implementation, or 10% of the expected net financial benefit over a period of up to five years, subject to an overriding maximum of £5,000.

- **Gifts & Entertainment** costing £100 or less provided by someone other than your employer i.e. supplier or client, assuming it must not have been organised by your employer or granted as an inducement.

- **Transport Costs** to take you home if you are occassionally required to work late (9pm or later) and public transport between your place of work and home has ceased or it would be unreasonable for your employer to expect you to use it.

- **Christmas Party** or another function of a similar nature costing no more than £50.00 per head and which is open to all staff.

EXPENSES ALLOWED BY STATUTE

- **Canteen Meals** provided for staff generally.
- **Contributions to Approved Occupational Pension Schemes.**
- **Membership Subscription**s to approved professional bodies but not fees.
- **Capital Allowances** in respect of capital equipment used in the course of the duties of your employment, including a private car.
- **Interest on Loans** to finance the purchase of capital equipment (including a private car) qualifying for capital allowances, but only for interest paid in the tax year in which the loan is taken out and in the three following years.
- **The cost of necessary medical treatment** abroad where an employee falls ill or suffers injury while away from the UK in the performance of his duties, and insurance for the employee against the cost of such treatment.
- **The Provision of Living Accommodation** by reason of an individual's employment.
- **Removal Expenses** paid by your employer where you have to change your residence on joining your employer or on transfer to another location within your organisation (maximum £8,000 per move).
- **Retraining courses** paid for an employee who is about to leave his employment or has left within the previous year to assist him in getting another job.
- **The Provision of a Car Parking Space** at or near the employee's place of work.
- **Flat-Rate Expenses** which have been agreed by the Inland Revenue and trade unions and professional associations.
- **Special Clothes** needed for work.
- **Supplies and Services** which are provided to you in your employer's business premises and used by you solely in performing your duties.
- **Security Services'** costs which are provided because of the nature of your job.
- **Business Entertainment** paid by you out of your gross pay, or out of your round-sum expense allowance, where the expenditure has been incurred wholly, exclusively and necessarily in the performance of your duties.
- **Nursery/Creche** facilities provided by the employer.
- **Goods and Services** which are provided at no cost to the employer.
- **Welfare, Sports and Social Facilities** which are provided by the employer.

OTHER TAX FREE INCOME

- Returns on National Savings Certificates.
- The first £70 of interest per person per year on the National Savings Ordinary Account
- Premium Bonds Prizes
- Lottery Winnings
- Income from scholarships (except certain company scholarships).
- Wedding and certain other presents from your employer that are not given in return for your services as an employee.
- Students grants you receive from a local authority.
- All returns on Save As You Earn (SAYE) savings schemes. These schemes were abolished with effect from 30th November 1994. Existing SAYE schemes will not be affected.
- Interest earned on Tax Exempt Special Savings Accounts (TESSAs) providing capital is not withdrawn during a five-year term and the maximum annual or investment conditions are not breached.
- Personal Equity Plans - dividend income under plans taken out after 6th April 1989 provided various conditions and limits are met.
- Life assurance policies - the proceeds of qualifying policies paid out at death or after a set number of years.
- Winnings on the football pools ,the National Lottery, and other forms or betting (although you may have to pay betting tax).
- Annuities paid to holders of certain gallantry awards.
- Bounty payments to members of the armed forces who voluntarily extend their service.
- Armed Services mess and ration allowances, Allowances, warrants and vouchers for travel on leave.
- Statutory redundancy pay.
- First £30,000 of compensation for loss of employment.
- Many disability pensions.
- Christmas bonuses from the Government to retirement pensioners.
- Lower rate allowances contining to be paid under the former Job Release Scheme.
- First 12 months' benefit under private sickness insurance policies.
- Friendly Society sickness and disability benefits and most sickness benefits under personal insurance policies.

- Youth Training Scheme (YTS) allowances including sick pay and Employment Training weekly allowance (including supplement and expense payments.
- Job Finders Grants. If you have been unemployed for two years or more you can get a job finder grant of £200 tax free.
- Vaccine damage payments.
- Most social security benefits.
- Child Adoption Allowance under approved schemes.

CAPITAL GAINS TAX

Capital Gains Tax (CGT) is a tax on gains arising on the disposal of capital assets.

Persons Chargeable: All persons resident in the UK for tax purposes are liable to the tax. Individuals who are resident and domiciled in the UK are chargeable on all gains wherever arising, while those who are resident and non-domiciled in the UK are liable only on non-UK gains to the extent that the gains are remitted to the UK.

Chargeable Assets: All forms of property are assets for CGT purposes e.g. options, debts and foreign currencies, except those specifically exempted.

Disposal: A disposal for CGT takes place whenever the ownership of an asset changes. This includes a part-disposal, even where no payment is received e.g. a gift or exchange. An exception to this latter rule is on death. In the case of death, no chargeable disposal takes place and the person who receives the asset is treated as having acquired it at the market value at the date of the death.

EXEMPTIONS AND RELIEFS
Annual Allowance
The first £6,000 of chargeable gains arising to you in the 1995/96 tax year is exempt from capital gains tax (£5,800 in 1994/95).

Private Residence
Normally, no capital gains tax arises on the disposal of your sole or main private residence and grounds up to half a hectare, provided it has been 'occupied' by you throughout the period of ownership.

However, capital gains which you are deemed to have made while you were living away from your sole or main home may be liable to capital gains tax, for example, if you rented your home for 5 years out of the 10 years you owned it, only half the gain would be exempt. However, certain periods of absence are regarded as periods of occupation, for example:

- If you cannot move into your new home within the first year because of alterations or because you could not sell your old home.
- Absences before the 31st March 1982.
- Periods during which you were away from your home because of your job up to a maximum of four years, or indefinitely if you are in job related accommodation.
- Period of absence whilst working full time overseas.
- Normally, absences for any reason totalling up to three years, as long as you use the home as your sole or main residence for some time both before the first period of absence and after the last one.
- The last three years of ownership before you sell your home are exempt, provided the property was at some time your sole or main residence.

Other Assets

The following are normally exempt from capital gains tax:

- Private Cars.
- National Savings Certificates, Premium Bonds, Capital Bonds and SAYE Deposits.
- British money, including post- 1837 gold sovereigns.
- Currency for personal use abroad.
- Betting winnings including pools, lotteries , horses and premium bonds.
- British Government stocks and most corporate bonds, if acquired after the 13th March 1984.
- Shares, unit trusts and investment trusts held in a PEP.
- Shares in qualifying Venture Capital Trusts.
- Shares issued after the 18th March 1986 under the Business Expansion Scheme which are sold more than five years after purchase.
- The proceeds from life insurance policies, provided you did not buy them from a third party.
- Damages for wrong or injury suffered in your private or professional life.
- Debts.
- A gain on the disposal of an award for valour or gallant conduct, provided it is sold by the original recipient.
- Gifts to charities or certain national institutions.
- A gift of heritage property, if certain conditions are satisfied.
- Any chattel which has a predictable useful life of no more than 50 years when you first acquired it, e.g. electronic equipment, yachts and race-horses, provided that you had not used the asset in your business so that it qualified for capital allowances.

- For chattels with a predictable life of more than 50 years, gains may be partly tax-free. Broadly speaking, if the disposal proceeds are less than £6,000, the gain is tax-free.
- Woodlands.

Married Couples

Before the 6th April 1990, a married couple got a £5,000 capital gains tax exemption. Now with the introduction of independent taxation from 6th April 1990, each spouse is entitled to a separate annual exemption. In 1995/96 this exemption is £6,000. The spouse who receives the asset is deemed to have acquired it on the date and at the cost at which the other spouse acquired it, unless the parties are separated or divorced. The capital losses of one spouse can no longer be offset against the gain of the other, including capital losses brought forward from the 6th April 1990.

Hold-Over Relief

No CGT is payable on gifts made before the 14th March 1989. After this date the relief is available in respect of:

- business assets
- gifts which count as chargeable transfers for inheritance tax purposes (mainly gifts to companies and certain types of discretionary trusts).

By claiming hold-over relief, the gain is passed on to the recipient, who is then taxed on the basis of the original market value when he/she disposed of the asset.

Example:

In June 1991, Anne gave her sister Julia shares in XYZ Ltd. valued at £13,000. Anne bought these shares in January 1989, for £10,000. They claimed hold-over relief. In April 1995 Julia sold the shares for £19,000. Julia's gain (ignoring indexation) after claiming hold-over relief is £9,000 (£19,000 - £10,000 and not £19,000 - £13,000).

The donor and the UK resident recipient must claim the hold-over relief within six years of the tax year in which the gift was made.

Gifts made after the 14th March 1989

The CGT may be paid in ten annual instalments where the gift is land, a controlling shareholding in a company or shareholdings in an unquoted company. Interest is charged on the unpaid tax.

Roll-Over Relief

Tax may be deferred, if the proceeds from the sale of business assets are reinvested in similar assets within 12 months before, or three years after the sale. The 1994 Budget extended roll over relief to all capital gains made after 29th November 1994 provided the proceeds are re-invested in Enterprise Investment Companies within 6 months of the capital gain being realised.

Tax Rate

Net chargeable gains are added to your taxable income and charged to capital gains tax at your appropriate income tax rate.

INHERITANCE TAX

Inheritance tax replaced the old system of capital transfer tax in March 1986. Inheritance tax may be payable on the value of your assets on death or gifts made in the seven years preceding your death or on life time gifts to certain trusts.

GIFTS FREE OF INHERITANCE TAX, WHETHER MADE DURING LIFE OR ON DEATH Gifts between a husband and wife are always free of inheritance tax, even where the couple are legally-separated but not divorced. However, gifts in excess of £55,000 from a spouse domiciled in the UK to a spouse not domiciled in the UK are taxable. Gifts made to recognised charities or political parties are free of inheritance tax.

GIFTS FREE OF INHERITANCE TAX ON DEATH ONLY

- Pension lump sums paid on your death, provided the trustees of the scheme have discretion over the beneficiaries.
- Estates of individuals killed on active military service, or whose death was brought about by such service are also free of inheritance tax.

GIFTS FREE OF INHERITANCE TAX IN LIFETIME ONLY

- Gifts made to individuals and some trusts more than seven years before your death. (Potentially Exempt Transfers)
- Gifts not exceeding £250 per year to any individual.
- Certain gifts 'in consideration of marriage'.
- The first £3,000 of any other gift in any year.
- Regular gifts made out of your normal income.

CALCULATION OF INHERITANCE TAX ON DEATH For transfers made on or after the 6th April 1995 the first £154,000 attracts inheritance tax at zero rate and the balance is charged at 40%. For transfers made between the 10th March 1992 and the 5th April 1995 the first £150,000 attracts inheritance tax at zero rate and the balance is charged at 40%. Prior to 10th March 1992 the zero rate applied to the first £140,000.

TAPERING RELIEF ON GIFTS Inheritance tax payable on potentially exempt transfers made between three and seven years before your death is reduced in accordance with the following scale:

Years Between Gift and Death	% of Inheritance Tax Payable
0 - 3	100%
3 - 4	80%
4 - 5	60%
5 - 6	40%
6 - 7	20%

The tax due on the lifetime gifts caught by the seven-year rule must be paid by the donees. The inheritance tax due on your estate is the responsibility of your executor or personal representative.

MAKING A WILL

When you make a will you express your wishes as to how your estate is to be disposed of when you die. You also appoint an executor to carry out your wishes and to distribute your assets to named beneficiaries.

Inheritance tax is due six months after the end of the month in which your death occurs. Your executor/personal representative must identify your assets and complete a nine-page Inland Revenue affidavit and pay the inheritance tax bill before probate will be granted.

HOW TO MAKE A WILL A will is a highly-important document and should be prepared by a Solicitor. If drawn up without legal assistance, a will can cause endless arguments and expense, and may have results very different from what were intended by you.

Before approaching a Solicitor you should:
- Decide who is to benefit under your will.
- Arrange who your executor will be, with his/her consent. Your executor will normally be one of your family, a close friend or business associate.

124

Note: Your executor is not required by law or code of practice to keep your beneficiaries informed or to consult with them about the manner in which your will is administered, so, be careful whom you choose. Banks, solicitors and other professions sometimes tend to charge excessive fees if they are appointed executor so check details in advance.

It is also important that your next of kin, executor or personal representative should know where all **your important documents** can be found, for example:

- Your Will
- Birth Certificate
- Marriage Certificate(s)
- Medical Card
- Pension Benefit
- Life Assurance Policies
- Investment Record details
- Important business papers
- Cash Deposit Accounts.

THREE POINTS REGARDING WILLS

- Your will must be in writing and must bear your signature at the end.
- Your will must be witnessed by two persons, neither of whom can be beneficiaries.
- You cannot entirely disinherit your spouse.

ADVANTAGES OF MAKING A WILL

- By making a will you ensure that your assets pass to the people of your choice.
- You are able to nominate the person whom you wish to act as your executor.
- You can 'guesstimate' the amount of inheritance tax payable on your death.

HOW LONG DOES A WILL LAST? Your will remains in force until your death except in the following cases:

- where a new will is made, this automatically revokes any previous will or wills you may have made.
- on marriage a will is revoked, unless it has clearly been made with the marriage in mind; on divorce your will is also automatically revoked.

SEPARATION / DIVORCE

A bequest to a former spouse under your will is automatically revoked on divorce. However, should you die after the date of your separation but prior to the decree absolute, any bequests to your former spouse will stand, unless you had executed a new will after your permanent separation commenced.

CHILDREN   Have you ever thought what might happen to your children if both you and your spouse were dead?

With a will, you can name your preferred guardian to look after your children's needs until they reach maturity. Without a will, your children may become wards of court until they become of age.

PROVISION FOR FAMILY AND DEPENDANTS ACT 1975 Sometimes, people leave a member of their family or a dependant relative out of their will - either deliberately or through forgetfulness. Anyone who can prove that they were partly or wholly maintained by you, can claim reasonable provision from your estate after your death whether a will exists or not, under the provisions of the Family and Dependants Act 1975.

Common-law spouses obtain no benefit under the intestacy rules. They can, however, apply to a court for 'reasonable provision' after your death. The procedure for claiming is both complicated and costly, so it is better to clearly think out your will in advance and so avoid disputes after you have gone.

TRUSTS Trusts are independent legal bodies set up to manage assets on behalf of 'beneficiaries'. They are set up by a person known as a 'settlor' and are administered by 'trustees'.

The advantages of setting up a trust may be administrative or they may be used as a vehicle for looking after someone close to you during your lifetime or after your death. There may also be tax advantages in setting up trusts. Property may be used for the benefit of your family without its being owned by any individual person or persons thus resulting in less tax being paid.

The 'settlor' sets out his/her wishes in a 'trust deed' and the 'trustees' manage the trust in accordance with these wishes.

GRANT OF PROBATE OR LETTERS OF ADMINISTRATION

When a person dies testate, it is necessary for the executor to obtain a Grant of Probate. Similarly, when a person dies intestate, it is necessary for the personal representative of the deceased to obtain a grant of Letters of Administration. Without one or other of these, it will not be possible to distribute your estate to your beneficiaries.

TESTATE AND INTESTATE A person who dies having made a will is said to have died Testate, and a person who dies having made no will is said to have died Intestate.

Died Intestate

The following chart outlines who gets what if you die *intestate* in England or Wales.

Relatives Surviving	Distribution of Estate where the Deceased died Intestate.
Spouse and Issue	Spouse is entitled to chattels and first £75,000, plus life interest in half of residue. Issue entitled to remaining half.
Spouse and No Issue	All the chattels and first £125,000 of rest of estate plus half of residue. Other half passes to deceased's parents or to brothers or sisters or to their children if parents are dead.
Issue and No Spouse	Estate divided equally. Children of dead issue take their parent's entitlement.
Father, Mother, Brothers and Sisters	One half to each parent.
Parent, Brothers and Sisters	Whole estate to parent.
Brothers and Sisters	All take equal shares. Children of a deceased brother or sister take their parent's share.
Grandparents	Shared equally.
Aunts and Uncles	All take equal shares.
No Next of Kin	Estate passes to the crown.

"The path of least resistance is what makes rivers run crooked.

Elbert Hubbard

PART FOUR

A Step by Step Guide to

COMPLETING YOUR ANNUAL TAX RETURN

OTHER DOCUMENTS YOU MAY NEED BEFORE COMPLETING YOUR TAX RETURN

Before you complete a tax return you may need other back-up documents, so the following list may give you some guidance.

1. **Employments, Pensions**

   If you were in employment, you will receive Form P60 in April each year, outlining your earnings and tax paid for the previous tax year. If your employment ceased before the end of the tax year, you will receive Form P45.

2. **Benefits/Expenses Allowances**

   You will need a copy of the Form P11D, filled in by your employer.

3. **Unemployment Benefit / Income Support**

   You will require a statement from your Benefit Office.

4. **Trade / Profession or Vocation**

   You will need your business accounts.

5. **Property in the UK**

   Summary of rental income arising and a statement of allowable expenses.

6. **UK Interest Not Taxed Before Receipt**

   Here you will need your passbooks for National Savings Investments and Certificates of Income from other sources.

7. **Interest Treated as Taxed Before Receipt / Dividends**

   You will need Bank/Building Society interest statements, share dividends and unit trust distribution counterfoils.

8. **Settlements**

   You will need Form R185 or Form R185E, if you get maintenance payments or alimony, or income from a trust or from the estate of someone who has died. You will need Form R185AP if you receive covenant payments.

9. **Outgoings: Expenses in Employment**

   You will need receipts for expenses in employment and allowable professional fees and subscriptions.

10. **Interest on Loans for the purchase or Improvement of Property in the UK**

    Certificates of interest will be required, if the interest has been paid gross or if you are a higher-rate taxpayer.

11. **Capital Gains**

    You will need contract notes for share dealings, and records for any other transactions that may give rise to capital gains tax.

FORM P1

INCOME AND CAPITAL GAINS 1995/96

This is a statement of income for the past year (1994/95) and a claim for your tax-free allowances for the current year (1995/96).

You will find a Form P1 reproduced on the following pages together with appropriate cross references to the relevant pages of this Guide for back-up information.

Inland Revenue

1994 Tax Return

H M Inspector of Taxes	Date of issue	Tax reference	National Insurance number
R. A. MacLaren	01/01/95	123/XY 9876	UK. 12. 12. 342

Tax Office address

Slough 2,
102- 104 Farnham Road
Slough
Berks   SL1 4YT

Jack Smith
200, Kings Road
Berks SL5 4YS

What you must do with this form

You are required by law to fill in this form, sign the declaration on page 4 and send the form, and any documents asked for, back to me within 30 days.

If you don't and there is no good reason for sending this form in late, you may have to pay a penalty. You may also have to pay interest on any tax paid late because this form was not sent back in time.

However the Inland Revenue will not seek interest simply because of delay provided that the return is sent back by 31 October 1994 (or within 30 days of issue if it was sent to you after 2 October 1994). For further information please refer to the introduction in the enclosed leaflet *"Filling in your 1994 Tax Return"*, which you should use in completing this form.

What details should you give ?

You only need to fill in the sections which apply to you.

Give amounts in the Income and Deductions column and details as requested in the Details column. You may use as much of the space as

you need for each item. Use a separate sheet of paper if you need more room.

You should show all the income and capital gains on which you may be charged to tax. Give details for the tax year which started on 6 April 1993 and ended on 5 April 1994 (1993-94) unless the form asks for something different.

You can also use this form to claim expenses and deductions for 1993-94 and personal allowances for the tax year which started on 6 April 1994 and ends on 5 April 1995 (1994-95).

If there is not enough space for your entries please give details on a separate sheet of paper.

Do you need help ?

If you need help please contact your Tax Office. The address and telephone number are shown above. You will need to quote your tax reference - *see above.*

Notes

See note 1

See the form P60 from your employer and note 2.

See note 3.

See note 4. Do not include expenses from self-employment.

See note 5.

See note 6.

See note 7.

You may be able to claim a deduction. See note 8.

See note 9. Do not claim relief already given.

P1 (1994)

Earnings etc 1993-94

	Income and (deductions)	Details
Wages, salary, fees or bonuses etc Give your occupation and most recent employer's name and address.	£	See page 136
Casual earnings, tips, expense allowances Give type of work and employer's name(s).	£	See page 139
Employment expenses for which you wish to claim Give type of expenses you wish to claim for.	(£)	See page 150/151
Lump sum and compensation payments not included above	£	See page 136
Approved profit sharing schemes Tick if you received a taxed sum. Give scheme name.		See page 137/138
Benefits in kind Tick if you receive any and state what they are. Give taxable values if you know them.	£	See page 139/141
Income from self-employment Turnover Allowable expenses £ (£) Profit (This is your turnover less allowable expenses)	£	See page 153/154 155/156/157
Work abroad Tick here if you were abroad for all or nearly all of a 365-day period beginning or ending during 1993-94 and you worked during that period.		See page 151/152
Trade union or friendly society death benefit and superannuation schemes Give amount relating to death or superannuation benefits and name of trade union or friendly society.	(£)	See page 183

1

Pensions and benefits for 1993-94

	Income	Details
Amount of State pension you were entitled to	£	See page 158
Widowed mother's allowance, invalid care allowance and industrial death benefit you were entitled to	£	See page 159
Other pensions received Give amount and the name and address of the payer.	£	See page 158
Unemployment benefit, or income support claimed because you were unemployed. Tick here and give name of your benefit office.	☐	See page 159

See note 10 for what counts as a State pension and other details.

See the form P60 from the payer.

Ask for "Income Tax and the Unemployed" (leaflet IR41).

Pensions you currently receive or expect to receive before 6 April 1995

Giving this information now will help ensure the right amount of tax is deducted. See note 10 for what counts as a State pension.

If not currently receiving the pension, date you expect it to start	Tick if a State pension	If currently receiving a pension, whether you receive it weekly, monthly, every 4 weeks or every 3 months	Amount you currently receive each time	Tick if this is after tax
/ /19		See page 158	159	☐
/ /19			£	

Other income

See note 11 for income you do not need to include. See note 12 for joint savings and investments.

National Savings

	Gross income	Details
Ordinary Account The first £70 of interest is exempt but should be included.	£	See page 164
Investment Account, Deposit Bonds, Income Bonds and Capital Bonds. Give the type of investment.	£	

	Net interest after tax	Tax deducted	Gross interest before tax
First Option Bonds Give the amount you received as shown on your tax certificate.	£	£	£

Other interest from UK banks, building societies etc.

The payer can supply the details you need. See note 13.

Give name of the bank, building society or other source (tick the box if you have registered to have interest paid gross)

Income after tax (leave blank if no tax was deducted)	Tax deducted (leave blank if no tax was deducted)	Gross income
£ See page 164	165	£
£	£	£

Dividends from shares in UK companies and income from unit trusts

See your statement or voucher and note 14. If you have not received a unit trust voucher ask your unit trust manager.

If your voucher shows a tax credit give the tax credit and the dividend. If your voucher shows tax deducted give the tax deducted and the gross income. Include unit trust income reinvested in units. See page 166 | 167

Name of the company or unit trust	Tax credit or tax deducted	Dividend	Gross income
	£	£	£
	£	£	£

Income from furnished rooms in your only or main home (UK only)

Under the Rent-a-Room scheme, £3,250 (or £1,625 if someone else is letting rooms in your home) of income from furnished rooms in your only or main home in the UK can be tax free. See note 15.

Tick one of the boxes below.

Your gross income was no more than £3,250 (or £1,625 if appropriate) and you do not opt out of the Rent-a-Room scheme. You do not need to give any more details. See page 159 | 160

Your gross income was more than £3,250 (or £1,625 if appropriate) and you want to be assessed on the difference between the rents and this amount, with no claim for expenses.

	Tax-free amount: (£3,250 or £1,625)	Gross income
	(£)	£

Neither of the above apply. Your rental income and expenses will be treated in the normal way. Give details under *Other income from property in UK or abroad*.

Other income from property in UK or abroad

See note 16 for expenses you can claim.

	Income	Details
In the Details column give address of property including the country (if not UK), type of let (furnished, unfurnished, of land, ground rents etc), gross income including profits from supplying gas or electricity, and expenses.		See page 160	161
Income less expenses	£	

Foreign investment income

See note 17.

Give the source and country.	£	See page 167

Maintenance and alimony you received

Give date of original order or agreement and of any further order or agreement since 15 March 1988. Tick here if you wish to claim the exemption.	£	See page 171	173

See note 18. Up to £1,720 may be exempt from tax: see note 19.

Income from trusts or settlements funded by others

Give name of trust or settlement and the amount of gross income received in the year	£	See page 170	171

See note 20.

Income from estates

Give name of deceased person and nature of your entitlement.	£	See page 171

See note 21.

All other income

Give the source.	£	See page 173

2

Deductions: legally binding maintenance or alimony payments

Give amount you were ordered to pay in 1993-94 **See page** |183 |£ 184 | 185)

Give amount you actually paid (if different). (£)

If your order/agreement is dated after 14 March 1988, give the date of any earlier order/agreement it varies, replaces, or revives. / /19

Date of your current order/agreement. / /19

Tick here if the payments are to your ex-husband/wife and he/she has remarried.

Tick if in the 1994-95 tax year you will be making payments to the Department of Social Security for your separated or divorced husband/wife, or children of the marriage, under a court order or Child Support Agency assessment.

Deductions: mortgage or loan for main home

Give name of lender. If the lender is a building society, give account number.

See page |174|175| 176 |177

If the lender is not a building society, give gross amount of interest paid in 1993-94. (£)

If the loan is not in the MIRAS scheme and not from a **building society** enclose a form Miras 5 or other certificate of interest paid from your lender. Tick here if you want your certificate returned.

Husband and wife: interest relief split
If you are married and you and your husband/wife want to change the way you share mortgage interest relief, tick and we will send you a form on which you can do this.

Other deductions

Other loans qualifying for tax relief
Only give details of loans not included elsewhere on this form. Give name of lender and purpose of loan. If for rental property, give number of weeks let during the tax year. Enclose a certificate of interest paid from your lender. (£)

Deductions	Details
	See page 177

Gift aid donations and covenants to charity
Give name of charity and date of any deed of covenant. (£) See page 186

Other covenants, settlements etc.
Give name of the person you pay and date of the deed. (£) See page 186

Payments abroad

Give the gross amounts of any payments of rent on UK property or yearly interest which you make to someone who normally lives abroad. £ See page 194

Capital gains 1993-94

Tick here if the total value of the assets you have disposed of in 1993-94 was more than £11,600.

Tick here if your chargeable gains were more than £5,800.

If you tick either box, give details of the assets and the gain (or loss) on each asset. If you need help contact your Tax Office. See page 188

£

Claim for personal tax allowances for 1994-95

You will be given the basic personal allowance automatically. You may claim other allowances below.

Allowances for those born before 6 April 1930
You may be able to claim a higher amount of personal allowance if you were born before 6 April 1930.

See page 195

Tick here to make your claim.

Allowances to be claimed by married men.
Married couple's allowance
Tick the relevant box to claim

See page 195

Give your wife's full name

You are living with your wife.

You separated from your wife before 6 April 1990 but are still married to her and have wholly maintained her since the separation with voluntary payments for which you are not entitled to any tax relief.

If you married after 5 April 1993 give the date of your marriage / /19

If you or your wife were born before 6 April 1930

See page 196

If you are entitled to the married couple's allowance you can claim a higher amount of allowance if you or your wife were born before 6 April 1930. **Tick here** to claim.

If your wife was born before 6 April 1930, give her date of birth / /19

3

Notes

See note 32.

If your wife is unable to look after herself
You may be able to claim the additional personal allowance if you are living with your wife who is totally incapacitated because of disability or illness and you have a child living with you.

Give details of the child for whom you are claiming under *If you have a child and are single, separated, divorced or widowed* below

See page 196
Give your wife's illness or disability

Tick here if your wife is likely to be unable to look after herself throughout the tax year ending on 5 April 1995.

See note 34.

See note 31.

Married couples

Allocation of married couple's allowance
A husband is responsible for claiming the married couple's allowance, but if you are living together you may choose how the allowance is to be allocated between you.
For 1995-96 one of you can ask for half the basic allowance to be given to each of you or jointly you can ask for all the basic allowance to be given to one of you.

Ask your Tax Office for 'A Guide for Married Couples' (leaflet IR80). See note 36 for blind persons allowance.

Transfer of surplus allowances to your wife or husband
To transfer any surplus allowances you must have been married and living with your wife or husband at any time in 1994-95. If you did not have enough income tax liability to use all (or any) of your married couple's allowance then you may transfer the surplus to your wife or husband.

Tick here if you need a transfer notice form.

See page 197
Tick here if you wish to do this
and you will be sent a form.
(You do not have to complete a form if you want the allocation for 1994-95 to continue in 1995-96).

See page 197
If you have insufficient income to use all (or any) blind person's allowance you are entitled to then you may transfer any surplus to your wife or husband. If you are a husband who does not have sufficient income to use his personal allowance in some circumstances your wife may receive transitional allowance.

See note 35 for details.

Allowance for widows

You may be able to claim for the year your husband died and the following year. **Tick here** to claim this allowance.

Give the date of your husband's death   /   / 19
See page 198

If you have a child and are single, separated, divorced or widowed

See notes 32 and 33 for more details.

You may be able to claim the additional personal allowance if you have a child living with you for all or part of the year and are single, separated, divorced or widowed for all or part of the year.

Details of the child
Give the name of the youngest child for whom you can claim

See page 199/200
Give the child's date of birth   /   / 19

If the child was 16 or over on 6 April 1994 and in full-time education or training give the name of the university, college or school or type of training.

See note 34 for details of shared claims.

Tick here to confirm the child lives with you.

Shared claims
Complete this item if:
• another person is claiming for the child named above **or**
• you live together as husband and wife with someone you are not married to who is also entitled to this allowance.

Give the other persons's (or your partner's) name and address

See page 200
State how you want the allowance to be shared (eg equally)
If you cannot agree how you want the allowance shared **between you,** give the number of days in the tax year that the child lives with you and the number of days the child lives with the other person.

See note 36.

Blind person's allowance

Tick here to claim the allowance.

Give the name of the Local Authority or equivalent body with which you have registered your blindness.

See page 200
The date you registered   /   / 19

Personal details

National Insurance number (if not as on front of this form)

Change of address. If you no longer live at the address shown on the front of this form, give your current address.

Date of birth (if you were born before 6 April 1935.)   /   /

Marital status. State if you are single, married, widowed, separated or divorced.

Declaration

You should keep a copy of your completed form or make entries in the boxes in the leaflet 'Filling in your 1994 Tax Return'.

You must sign this statement. If you give false information or conceal any part of your income or chargeable gains, you can be prosecuted.

The information I have given on this form is correct and complete to the best of my knowledge and belief.

Signature *See page 200*

Date   /   / 19

4

Printed in the UK for HMSO 1/94 Dd 8407667 2804M 25038

TAX RETURN 1995 - FORM 11P
(Model Form Page 204)

This tax return is normally completed by employees who earn in excess of £8,500 p.a..

It can be subdivided into four main sections:

- Income for the past tax year 1994/95.
- Outgoings and allowable deductions for the past tax year 1994/95.
- Capital gains for the past tax year 1994/95.
- Claims for tax-allowances and reliefs in the current tax year 1995/96.

INCOME FROM EMPLOYMENT ETC.

Here you are required to give full details of your gross earnings before tax for duties performed wholly in the UK. Earnings include, statutory sick pay, statutory maternity pay, income tax paid by your employer on your behalf and not deducted from your pay and earnings as an agency worker.

Show the income before expenses, but after superannuation contributions, payroll-giving donations and profit-related pay relief have been deducted.

Your earnings for the year will be stated on your Form P60, which you get from your employer in April each year.

From the 6th April 1989, the amount to be included for director's remuneration is the amount actually received or treated as received in the tax year - which may be the figure on your Form P60 or salary or fees shown in your company accounts, even if they were not actually paid.

LUMP SUM AND COMPENSATION PAYMENTS

When you leave employment, you will normally be due some or all of the following: normal wages, pay in lieu of holidays, pay for work done during your notice period, outstanding commission etc. All of these payments are taxed in the normal way under PAYE, with the exception of the following, which are exempt:

- Any lump sum paid for injury or disability.
- Compensation for loss of employment completed entirely or substantially outside the UK.
- Certain lump sum benefits from your employer's pension scheme.
- Qualifying monies which your employer pays into a retirement benefit fund on your behalf.

Other payments may also be tax-free, if they do not exceed £30,000:

- redundancy payments made under the Government's redundancy payments scheme or a scheme approved by the Inland Revenue.
- pay in lieu of notice, provided your conditions of employment do not entitle you to it.
- other payments you may receive, provided they are not payments for work done and are 'unexpected'.

Payments in excess of £30,000, are added to your income and taxed in the normal way.

PROFIT-RELATED PAY (PRP)

If you belong to a profit-related pay scheme (PRP), give the scheme number here. From 1st April 1991 all of your profit-related pay under an approved profit-related scheme is tax-free up to the lower of:

- 20% of total pay or
- £4,000 p.a.
- the actual PRP received in the tax year.

Tax relief is given on PRP by your employer through the PAYE system. Your employer can deduct the whole of the PRP payments from taxable trading profits in the same way as ordinary salary payments.

The scheme must be registered and approved by the Inland Revenue (the Profit-Related Pay Office).

PROFIT SHARING

EMPLOYEE SHARE SCHEMES

Employee share schemes enable you to obtain a stake in your employer's business with considerable tax advantages provided the scheme is approved by the Inland Revenue.

Approved schemes normally fall under one of the following headings:

- Profit-sharing schemes.
- Share-option schemes.
- Savings-related share-option schemes.

137

PROFIT SHARING SCHEMES

Under an approved profit-sharing scheme, you can get shares in your employer's firm free of tax. The yearly value is £3,000 or 10% of your earnings, whichever is the higher, up to a maximum of £8,000 a year. An approved scheme must meet certain conditions. For example, the shares must be held in trust for at least two years, unless you die, reach retirement or are made redundant or you stop work through injury or disablement.

No income tax liability will arise on the sale of the shares if sold after five years from the date of acquisition, or earlier if you die. If there is a disposal of scheme shares before the release date (i.e. five years), income tax will be payable on a proportion of the original market value of the shares or the disposal proceeds, if less.

Period Held	% Tax Payable
2-3 Years	100
4 Years	75
5 Years	Nil

If you cease employment or reach retirement age, your taxable benefit is reduced by 50%.

Example:

In January 1991, Bob acquired shares to the value of £3,500 in his employer's profit-sharing scheme. He decided to sell them for the same value in March 1995. Bob is a higher-rate taxpayer.

Taxable Benefit -	£3,500 x .75%	=	£2,625
Tax Payable @ 40%		=	£1,050

SHARE-OPTION SCHEMES give you the right to acquire shares at a fixed price in your employer's company at some future date, but at today's market price. For a scheme to meet Inland Revenue approval it must satisfy the following conditions:

- The maximum amount of the option must be limited to £100,000 or four times your earnings in the year the option is granted or in the previous year, if this is greater.
- The price you pay for the shares cannot be less than the market value at the time of the option.
- You cannot excerise the option earlier than three years or later than ten years after it has been granted.
- You must work at least twenty hours a week for your employer or twenty-five hours if you are a director.

No income tax is payable when you exercise your option. However, some capital gains tax may be payable when you sell the shares.

From the 1st January 1992, if an employer operates an approved all-employee share scheme and meets certain other conditions the sales price of the shares may be set at a discount of up to 15% of market value without incurring any additional tax liability.

SAVINGS-RELATED SHARE-OPTION SCHEMES Under a savings-related share-options scheme, your company gives you the option to buy shares some time in the future, at a price fixed now. The funds to buy the shares are generated by a special Save-As-You-Earn scheme which can extend over five or seven years. To qualify, the scheme must normally meet the following conditions:
- Savings cannot exceed £250 a month or be less than £10 per month.
- The option price to buy shares cannot be less than 80% of the market value at the time the option is granted

No income tax is payable when you exercise your option to buy the shares. However, some capital gains tax may be payable on the disposal of the shares.

OTHER PAYMENTS RECEIVED

You should enter here payments such as cash-in-hand payments, casual earnings, tips etc.

CARS & CAR FUEL

For benefit-in-kind purposes taxpayers are divided into two categories:
- employees earning less than £8,500 p.a.
- employees earning more than £8,500 p.a. and directors.

A company car is not deemed to have any taxable benefit for lower-paid employees.

DINKY TOYS Ltd.
THE BENEFITS INCLUDE OF COURSE THIS COMPANY CAR
Tom Matthews

Company Cars

From 5th April 1994 the taxable benefit arising on company cars is based on the original list price of the car at the time it was first registered, up to a maximum amount of £80,000. The list price of the car includes delivery charges, standard accessories and optional extras (in excess of £100) added to the car after 31st July 1993.

BENEFIT IN KIND

The Benefit in Kind or taxable benefit is 35% of the list price of the car if your business mileage is less than 2,500 miles p.a.

If your business mileage is between 2,500 and 17,999 miles in a year the Benefit in Kind or taxable benefit is reduced by one third.

If your business miles is 18,000 or more in a year the taxable benefit is reduced by two thirds.

If your car is more than four years old at the end of the tax year the taxable benefit after any reduction for business mileage is further reduced by one third.

Private Use

If you make a contribution towards the private use of a company car this amount will reduce pound for pound the amount on which you pay tax.

Example:

Eric is provided with a 1990 company car by his employer. The car's original market value was £9,000 and Eric does 12,000 business miles per year. He reimburses his employer £100 for private use of the car.

Eric's Benefit in Kind is as follows:

£9,000 @ 35%	£3,150
Less: reduction for mileage 1/3	(£1,050)
	£2,100
Less: reduction for age of car 1/3	(£700)
	£1,400
Less: amount reimbursed	(£100)
BIK amount	£1,300

This Benefit in Kind will normally be deducted from Eric's PAYE Code. From 5th April 1995 accessories for the disabled added to a company car are not taxable.

Classic Cars with a Market Value in excess of £15,000

If your company car is more than 15 years old at the end of the tax year and it's current market value is in excess of £15,000 and also higher than the list price when the car was first registered, then the open market value of the car on the last day of the relevant tax year is the assessable amount for Benefit in Kind purposes.

Are people over 40 better drivers?

If you're over 40 you could well be entitled to a saving on your motor insurance with a Hibernian Motorwise policy. Why? Why Not?

You see, we reckon that mature motorists are better risks and Motorwise takes this into account by rewarding you for your good driving record.

For Motorwise you should be aged between 40 and 70, hold a full, clean driving licence, drive an approved car of up to Group 16 for social, domestic and pleasure use (in some cases limited business use) on which a minimum of 3 years no-claim discount has been earned.

Motorwise offers you a range of attractive options, benefits and discounts.

Ask your broker about Motorwise from Hibernian. After all, if you're a better driver don't you deserve a lower premium?

2/14 Shortlands, Hammersmith,
London W6 8DJ.
Telephone: (081) 7415051.

hi
HIBERNIAN
INSURANCE

BRISTOL • CHELTENHAM • GUILDFORD • HUNTINGDON • IPSWICH
LINCOLN • NEWPORT • PLYMOUTH • READING • SHREWSBURY
SOUTHAMPTON • TAUNTON • TRURO • TUNBRIDGE WELLS • WARE

Pool Cars

No taxable benefit arises on the use of a pool car. To qualify as a pool car:
- It must be used by more than one employee.
- It must not normally be kept overnight in the vicinity of an employee's home.
- Any private use of the car is only incidental to it's business use.

Car Fuel Benefit

If your employer provides free fuel for use in your private capacity, this benefit is taxable for petrol and diesel cars as follows in 1994/95:

	TAXABLE BENEFIT	
CAR	**PETROL**	**DIESEL**
Cylinder capacity		
up to 1,400 cc	£640	£580
1,401 to 2,000 cc	£810	£580
2,001 cc or more	£1,200	£750

If you reimburse your employer for the full cost of fuel used in your private capacity, or if your employer provides fuel only for business purposes, no taxable benefit will arise.

Mileage Allowance Paid by Employer

Where an employer pays a mileage allowance, rather than directly reimbursing the motoring costs which you incur on business use of your car, you should enter this amount on your tax return and claim the actual costs or expenses incurred as a deduction, unless your employer has a dispensation from the Inland Revenue to pay your mileage allowance tax-free.

Remember, from the 6th April 1990 you may claim as an expense:
- capital allowances and
- interest relief on a loan used to purchase your car.

But only in in respect of that proportion of these costs that are related to the business use of your car.

FIXED PROFIT CAR SCHEME

Also from the 6th April 1990, a fixed mileage allowance may be paid free of tax to all employees; the amount depends on your total business mileage and the engine size of your car. The following table sets out the rates from 6th April 1994.

ANNUAL MILEAGE	CAR ENGINE SIZE			
	Up to 1000 cc	1001 to 1500 cc	1,500 to 2000 cc	Over 2000 cc
Up to 4,000 p.a.	27p	33p	41p	56p
Over 4,000 p.a.	15p	19p	23p	31p

If your mileage rate is not linked to the car's engine size, the rates are 36p up to 4,000 miles p.a. and 20p for any additional mileage.

Company Vans

From 6th April 1993 if you are provided with a company van which is used for private travel you are liable to pay tax on this benefit. The BIK amount is a standard £500 p.a. where the van is less than 4 years old and £350 where the van is more than 4 years old.

OTHER BENEFITS IN KIND AND EXPENSE ALLOWANCES

Under the general tax law, some payments and benefits to employees are known as fringe-benefits and are taxable under Schedule E and PAYE.

For fringe-benefit purposes taxpayers are divided into two categories:
- Directors and employees earning more than £8,500 p.a.
- Employees earning less than £8,500 p.a.

Directors earning less than £8,500 p.a. who work full-time for the company and who, together with associates control less than 5% of the ordinary share capital of the company, may also be excluded from the director and employees earning more than £8,500 p.a.

The following are taken into account before determining whether you earn more or less than £8,500 p.a:
- Gross Pay, less superannuation contributions.
- All expense payments.
- All benefits, including a company car and car fuel 'scale charge' or any other benefits paid by vouchers and credit cards.

TAXABLE FRINGE-BENEFITS As a general rule, the taxable value of fringe-benefits is added to your earnings and taxed in the normal way. However, to render a benefit taxable it must be received by reason of employment and the taxable benefits are normally deducted on your notice of coding, so that they may be accounted for under PAYE.

VALUATION OF BENEFITS - EMPLOYEES EARNING LESS THAN £8,500 p.a.

The rule for this category of employee is that you are taxed on a fringe-benefit only if it is for money's worth or can be converted into money's worth. So, you are taxed on the 'net realizable value' or the second-hand value of the fringe-benefit.

Consequently, many fringe-benefits to lower-paid employees are tax-free. The following benefits are considered to have no redeemable value and are tax-free for employees earning less than £8,500 p.a.

- The use of a company car.
- Cost of private medical insurance.
- Board and lodging not paid by cash.
- Fees and subscriptions paid by way of membership of a society.
- Hairdressing services provided at work.
- Use of employer's property.
- Children's educational scholarships.

The second-hand value of certain items can be low. For example, if your employer gave you a video camera costing £500, its second-hand value could be as low as £300.

VALUATION OF BENEFITS - DIRECTORS + EMPLOYEES EARNING MORE THAN £8,500 P.A.

The general rule is that the value of a benefit provided for a director or employee earning more than £8,500 p.a. is its cash equivalent value or the marginal cost of the benefit to the employer.

The marginal cost of fringe benefit depends on each employer's particular circumstances, for example:

- no benefit will arise on rail or bus travel, used by employees provided you do not displace fare paying passengers or involve your employer in any additional costs.
- also if goods are sold at a discount which leave you paying at least the wholesale price, no benefit will arise.
- if a teacher pays 15% or more of the school's normal fees there is deemed to be no net taxable benefit.
- No taxable benefit will arise on professional service benefit provided no additional labour costs were involved by your employer and provided you meet the cost of any disbursements.

So, enter here the 'taxable value' of the benefits you get from your employer unless your employer has a dispensation from returning these benefits on Form P11D. Employers are obliged to give details of all the benefits and perks paid to employees on Form P11D, unless their earnings, expenses and benefits-in-kind are less than £8,500 p.a., or they have a dispensation from the Inland Revenue from so doing.

Many exceptions to this general rule exist; for example, living accommodation and share incentive schemes.

145

BENEFICIAL LOANS

If you or any of your relatives receive a cheap or interest free loan by reason of your employment, the benefit arising from such a loan may be taxable. Beneficial loans paid to employees who earn less than £8,500 are tax free.

QUALIFYING LOAN FOR INTEREST RELIEF

The benefit in kind on a loan which qualifies for interest relief is the difference between the amount of interet payable at the "official rate" and the amount of interet if any, which you actually paid. The "Official Rate" is fixed by way of a Treasury Order in line with typical mortgage rates. The official rate from 6th January 1994 was 7.5% and for the tax year 1993/94 was 7.688%. Interest relief is available on the amount of interest paid at the official rate rather than the actual amount of interest paid.

OTHER LOANS

If the loan does not qualify for interest relief a Benefit in Kind charge will not arise unless the loan is for more than £5,000 (£300 up to 1993/94). If it does exceed £5,000 the Benefit in Kind amount is calculated in the same way as a loan which qualifies for interest relief.

A loan incluces:

- Salary advances
- Credit facilities
- Arranging, guaranteeing or faciliting a third party loan.

Exemptions:

- Where an interest free or cheap loan is made to a relative and you can show that you have derived no personal benefit from the loan no charge to Benefit in Kind will arise.
- From 5th April 1994 no Benefit in Kind charge will arise to an employee if loans on similar terms are made available to the general public.

LOANS WRITTEN-OFF

If your employer writes-off a loan by reason of your employment, the amount written-off is taxable except:

- Where the loan is written-off under "stop-loss" arrangements relating to share incentive schemes entered into before 6th April 1976.
- Where the release of the loan follows the death of the employee.
- Where the loan written-off was to a relative and one from which you derived no benefit.

USE OF COMPANY-OWNED ASSETS

The taxable charge is the 'annual value of the use of the asset', or the rent or hire charge paid, if this is greater. Any additional expenses met by your employer in providing the asset are also included. The annual value is taken as 20% of the market value of the asset when it was first provided as a benefit. The annual value where the asset was first provided before 6th April 1980 is 10%.

LIVING ACCOMMODATION

If your employer provides you with living accommodation by reason of your employment, you may be liable to tax on this benefit. The tax charge is calculated by reference to the gross annual value (GAV) of the property occupied, less any rent paid. The annual value of the property is the gross rateable value or the rent paid by your employer, if this is greater. For properties which do not have a gross rateable value an amount is agreed between the Inland Revenue and your employer.

Note: By concession, the annual value of accommodation in Scotland will not be assessed on the 1985 rates revaluation. Instead the 1978 valuation will be used in assessing the annual value of accommodation for 1985/86 and 1986/87 and for subsequent years an annual value is calculated by scaling back the 1985 rating value.

ADDITIONAL TAX CHARGE arises if you are provided with living accommodation which costs in excess of £75,000. This £75,000 also includes the cost of improvements, less any contributions made by you. The additional tax charge is calculated by multiplying the excess of the cost (or deemed cost) of the property, including the cost of any improvements, over £75,000, by the 'official rate' of interest in force at the beginning of the tax year. Any rent paid by you is deducted before arriving at the taxable benefit.

Example:

You are provided with accommodation costing £200,000, the gross annual value (GAV) is £1,000. Let us assume that the Treasury rate of interest is 7.5%. The assessable benefit is

GAV	£1,000
Additional Charge	
£200,000 - £75,000 x 7.5%	£9,375
Net Assessable Benefit	£10,375

SUBSTITUTION OF MARKET VALUE FOR COST

If you first occupy living accommodation on or after 31st March 1983, the cost of which including improvements exceeds £75,000, and the property was acquired by the employer or a connected person more than six years before the date of first occupancy, market value at the later date is taken as the cost.

RUNNING COSTS such as heating, lighting and telephone, incurred by a director or higher-paid employee are also taxable, if these costs are paid by the employer. Similarly, tax arises on the provision of furniture and other assets, in accordance with the general rules governing employer-owned assets.

EXEMPTIONS TO ADDITIONAL TAX CHARGE

The tax charge is not levied if you live in 'representative occupation'. This exemption does not apply to directors unless they have no material interest (less than 5% shareholding) in the company and are full-time working directors. Directors of non-profit making companies or charities are excluded.

'REPRESENTATIVE ACCOMMODATION' occurs where you are required to reside in accommodation:

- For the proper performance of your duties, or
- For the better performance of your duties, or if your employment is one for which it is customary for employers to provide accommodation.
- The accommodation is provided for security reasons.

REPRESENTATIVE ACCOMMODATION FOR DIRECTORS + EMPLOYEES EARNING MORE THAN £8,500 P.A.

For directors and employees earning more than £8,500 p.a. who live in 'representative accommodation', the benefit arising from the use of furniture and effects, together with repair, maintenance, decoration, heating, lighting and cleaning costs etc. met by the employer is restricted to 10% of their emoluments.

Example:

Eric lives in 'Representative Accommodation' and his employer pays the following expenses:

Telephone, Heat and Light	£2,000
Gardener and Kitchen Staff	£10,000
Furnishings provided at Cost	£8,000
	£20,000

Eric's salary and assessable benefits-in-kind are £56,000. So, his taxable benefits on the expenses paid by his employer are restricted to £5,600 (£56,000 x 10%).

ASSETS TRANSFERRED TO AN EMPLOYEE

The taxable benefit is the difference between the amount, if any, paid by you for the asset and the higher of:

- the market value of the asset at the date of transfer or,
- the market value of the asset when first provided, less any sums already taken into account in taxing benefits deriving from the use of that asset.

Example:

On 6th April 1992, your employer provided you with the use of a computer costing £5,000. In December 1995 your employer sells the computer to you for £500. The open market value is £1,000.

Taxable Benefits

Year			Amount
1992/93	£5,000 X 20%		£1,000
1993/94	£5,000 X 20%		£1,000
1994/95	£5,000 X 20%		£1,000
Original Cost		£5,000	
Already Taxed	£3,000		
Cash Paid	£500	£3,500	
Taxable Benefit 1995/96			£1,500

CASH VOUCHERS

Cash vouchers, credit tokens, credit cards and charge cards etc. The taxable benefit is the cost to your employer in providing these vouchers etc.

WORKPLACE NURSERIES

From the 6th April 1990 the cost of workplace nurseries provided by your employer is a non-taxable benefit subject to certain conditions. You must be a parent or foster parent of the child and the care may not be provided on domestic premises. The nurserys must be run by your employer or your employer must participate in the cost and management of the nursery, or the nursery must be set up jointly with another employer, voluntary body, or local authority. Similar facilities provided for older children are also tax-free.

Cash payments or vouchers provided by your employer to pay for childcare facilities will continue to be taxable, as will the cost of childcare places bought in other employers' schemes, unless your employer becomes involved in the management of these schemes.

EXPENSES FOR WHICH YOU WISH TO CLAIM

Expenses in employment are only allowed as a deduction if they are 'wholly exclusively and necessarily incurred in performing your duties of employment or office'. Relief can be obtained through the PAYE system in the following tax year or by getting a tax rebate after you complete your annual tax return.

The following expenses would normally be tax-deductible.

Accommodation and Meal Expenses

Reasonable hotel accommodation and meal expenses incurred while travelling in the course of your employment and not reimbursed by your employer.

Books and Stationery

Cost of reference books and stationery not provided by your employer but which are necessary in the performance of your duties.

Clothes

Cost of replacing, cleaning and repairing protective and functional clothing necessary for your job and not provided by your employer.

Fees or Subscriptions to Professional Bodies

Fees which you are required to pay in order to carry on your job or profession. Subscriptions to certain professional bodies and societies are also allowable if their activities are relevant to your work. Enter only the part of the subscription which the society tells you is tax-deductible.

Flat-Rate Expenses

Special flat-rate expenses are allowed to certain categories of workers, such as teachers, nurses, journalists and building workers. These amounts are agreed from time to time between the Inland Revenue, and trades unions and professional bodies.

Home Expenses

You can claim a proportion of your heating, lighting, cleaning and insurance bills etc., provided it is necessary that you carry out some of your employment duties at or from your home.

Round-Sum Expenses

If you get a round-sum expense allowance from your employer, it will be regarded as part of your income and taxed, unless you can demonstrate that the expenses were incurred 'wholly, exclusively and necessarily' in the performance of your duties. If your expenses actually exceed the sums reimbursed, you are entitled to an expense allowance for the excess.

Tools, Instruments etc.

The cost of buying or replacing tools, musical instruments etc., including the cost of maintenance and repairs, unless your trade union has agreed a fixed deduction with the Inland Revenue for your particular industry.

Training

Cost of fees and essential books which you are required to buy on a full-time external training course lasting four weeks or more, provided your employer encourages you to attend this course and continues to pay your wages while you are on this course.

Travelling

The cost of travelling to and from work is not normally tax-deductible. However, travelling expenses incurred strictly in the course of your employment duties are tax-deductible, if they are not reimbursed by your employer. Also, remember, if your employer requires you to use your car for business purposes and pays you less for doing so than it costs you, you can claim the difference as a tax-deductible expense.

Interest

Interest on loans to purchase equipment which is necessary for your job.

EARNINGS FROM WORK ABROAD

A UK resident going abroad to work may be regarded as non-resident here for tax purposes, provided the duties of the employment are performed wholly outside the UK and the period of absence spans at least one complete tax year.

FOREIGN ASSIGNMENTS

Under this section, you can claim 100% relief from UK tax on earnings, even if you remain resident in the UK for tax purposes.

To claim this relief, you must have been working abroad for 365 days or more within a qualifying period.

You may be abroad for the whole of the qualifying period. Alternatively, you can return to the UK for short visits, provided no intervening period in the UK is longer than 62 days and the total number of days in the UK is not more than one-sixth of the total number of days in the qualifying period.

So you can have a succession of periods in the UK and abroad and still qualify for 100% tax deduction.

Example:

Charles worked abroad for his employer from the 3rd September 1993 to the 23rd February 1995. His trips to the UK and the number of days working abroad were as follows:

Location	Dates	No of Days
Abroad	From 03.09.93 to 11.12.93	100
UK	From 12.12.93 to 19.02.94	70
Abroad	From 20.02.94 to 07.07.94	139
UK	From 08.07.94 to 05.09.94	60
Abroad	From 06.09.94 to 23.02.95	171

His first trip to the UK breaks the 62 day rule, so the first 100 days abroad are excluded. The new qualifying period starts from the 20th February 1994. At the end of the third trip abroad, he has spent 60 days in the UK out of a total of 370.

This is a qualifying period, as his stay in the UK from the 8th July 1994 to the 5th September 1994 is less than 62 days and is also less than 1/6th of the total qualifying period.

So Charles's earnings abroad over this period qualify for 100% UK tax deduction.

Remittance Basis

If you are not domiciled in the UK but are resident and ordinarily resident here and work for an employer outside the UK, tax on a remittance basis may apply, provided no part of your duties, other than incidental duties relating to this overseas employment, are performed in the UK. See page 114 for details.

UK Residence

There are advantages in remaining a UK resident, even if you do not pay UK income tax:

- The full amount of your personal allowances may be claimed against other income, such as investment income.
- Double Taxation Relief may be claimed on foreign income.
- If you rented your home in the UK, the rental income would not suffer withholding tax.

INCOME FROM SELF-EMPLOYMENT

If you are self-employed and run a business, (outside a limited company) any profits you make should be entered here.

Do not enter in this section, any income arising from isolated or casual spare-time work which is not really a business. This is more appropriate to the section 'All other profits or income'.

If you are self-employed you must keep accurate records of all your business transaction. It will be easier if you record all your business earnings or sales as you make them and all your expenses as you incur them. Keep all bank or building society records, sales invoices, receipted bills etc. as well as records of your personal bank or building society accounts, especially if there have been transfers between your personal accounts and the business.

If your turnover was £15,000 or more you should send with your completed return a statement of your profit or loss for tax purposes for the accounting period, supported by detailed accounts.

The Inland Revenue has launched a free video and booklet to help people starting up in business, so that they do not run into problems with their tax. The 15 minute video "Getting Tax Right From The Start" and the supporting booklet gives simple seven step guide to tax basics. They are available at all Inland Revenue Tax Enquiry Centres, and at the Public Enquiry Room, Somerset House, London WC2.

What to Enter

On your Form 11P, you should enter the nature of your trade or business, the address and business name, if different from your own. Enter your profits for the accounting year ending within the year to 5th April 1995. Your profits should be adjusted for expenditure which is not allowable for tax purposes e.g.

- Capital expenditure and depreciation.
- Entertainment expenses.
- Personal expenses, such as private motoring, holidays etc.
- Drawings and Class 2NI Contributions.
- Political donations.
- Expenses which are not laid out wholly and exclusively for the purposes of the trade or profession.

If you started business during the year to the 5th April 1995, give the date you started and the date up to which your accounts will be made and write 'profits to be agreed'. If you started business before the 6th April 1995, and accounts will not be made up until a date in the year ending 1995, state the date up to which accounts will be made and write 'profits to be agreed'.

Note: If your turnover is greater than £15,000, all expenditure for business purposes should be properly documented. You should at least keep a cash book, a purchase book, a sales book and a petty cash book, together with all invoices and receipts. These receipts will be necessary, not only for preparing your accounts, but also for completing your VAT returns.

Only half of Class 4 National Insurance contributions are deductible from trading profits before arriving at total income. Trading profits for Class 4 purposes are usually the same as your income tax profits. However, there may be a difference if you can claim interest or loss relief. If you do have interest or loss relief claims, you should cross the box and give details on a separate sheet.

CAPITAL ALLOWANCE

Depreciation charges in your accounts are not tax-deductible. However, you can claim capital allowances. Claimed capital-allowances are referred to as writing-down allowances.

Writing-down allowances are given for the tax year in which your profits are taxed, not for the year in which the expenditure is incurred. Thus, capital expenditure arising in the accounts for the year ended 31st December 1994, will qualify for capital allowances in the tax year 1995-1996.

Reducing Balance

On some assets, the writing-down allowance is calculated as a fixed percentage of the reducing balance. For example:

Plant, machinery and equipment	25%
Fixtures and fittings	25%
Motor cars (maximum allowance £3,000 per year)	25%
Vans and lorries	25%
Office furniture and equipment	25%
Insulation of factories and warehouses	25%
Fire safety expenditure	25%

On other assets, the writing-down allowance is calculated on the original cost. For example:

Industrial buildings	4%
Agricultural buildings	4%
Hotel buildings	4%

For the first year capital allowances have been increased from 25% to 40% for all assets except motor cars. However, this only applies for the 12 months ending 31st October 1993.

Enterprise Zones

Under the enterprise-zone allowances, an initial alllowance of 100% on industrial and commercial building expenditure is tax-deductibe. Hotels may also qualify if they:

- have at least ten bedrooms for letting to the public
- provide breakfast and evening meals
- are open for at least four months between April and October.

Example:

Paul's trading profits for 1994/95 were £125,000. During that year, he purchased new industrial premises in an enterprise zone for £110,000 and spent £10,000 on plant and machinery.

	£	1995/96 £
Trading Profits		125,000
Less Capital Allowances 25%		
(Plant & Machinery)	2,500	
Enterprise-Zone Allowance	110,000	112,500
Taxable Profits		12,500

Capital Allowance - Pools

If you have more than one asset qualifying for capital allowances, they are put into a pool. Each year you may then calculate the writing-down allowance on the value of the pool.

Cars must be kept in separate pools.

Short-Life Assets

Short-life assets such as tools, may also be put in separate pools. When such assets are sold, you deduct from the pool the smaller of, the original cost of the asset or the money you received when you sold it. If you sell or scrap short-life assets which are part of a pool and the proceeds come to less than its pool value, you can deduct the difference from your annual profits.

BASIS OF ASSESSMENT - NEW BUSINESS commencement after 5th April 1994

Tax Year	Basis of Assessment:
First:	Actual profits from commencement to the following 5th April.
Second:	Profits for the first 12 months of trading.
Third:	Current years profits e.g. if your accounts year end is 31st December, your profits for the year ended 31st December 1996 will be taxed in the 1996/97 tax year.

BASIS OF ASSESSMENT - CESSATION OF BUSINESS

Tax Year	Basis of Assessment:
Final	Actual profits from the 6th April to date of cessation.
Penultimate (2nd last) and Pre-penultimate	Where the total profits of these two years taken together exceed the assessments as originally-based on the profits of the preceding year, then the assessment for each of the two years will be revised by the tax office to the actual profits to the 5th April in each year.
Example:	A trade commenced on the 1st July 1988 and ceased on the 30th September 1994. The adjusted profits for tax are as follows:

	£
6 months to 31.12.88	10,000
Year Ending 31.12.89	12,000
Year Ending 31.12.90	8,000
Year Ending 31.12.91	20,000
Year Ending 31.12.92	28,000
Year Ending 31.12.93	32,000
9 months to 30.09.94	27,000

	Year of Assessment	Basis of Assessment	Original Assessment	Final Assessment
	1988/89	01.07.88 to 05.04.89	£13,000	£13,000
(a)	1989/90	12 months to 30.06.89	£16,000	£11,000
(b)	1990/91	Year to 31.12.90	£12,000	£11,000
	1991/92	Year to 31.12.91	£8,000	£8,000
(c)	1992/93	Year to 31.12.92	£20,000	£29,000
(d)	1993/94	Year to 31.12.93	£28,000	£33,000
	1994/95	6.4.94 to 30.9.94	£18,000	£18,000

Commencement 2nd and 3rd years (a) and (b)
Note:

(a) - 2nd Year Claim
       The taxpayer may claim to have the assessment for 1989/90 reduced to
       the actual profits for 1989/90 i.e. year ending 5.4.90

£12,000 X 3/4	=	£9,000
£8,000 X 1/4	=	£2,000
		£11,000

(b) - 3rd Year Claim
       The taxpayer may claim to have the assessment for 1990/91 reduced to
       the actual profits for 1990/91 i.e. year ending 5.4.91

£8,000 X 3/4	=	£6,000
£20,000 X 1/4	=	£5,000
		£11,000

(c) and (d)

-      Penultimate and pre-penultimate years
       The Inspector will revise the assessment for both these years to actual
       profits (i.e. to 5th April) if the aggregate of the profits exceeds the total
       of the original assessments.

	1992/93	Actual Profits	Original Assessment
06.04.92 to 31.12.92 £28,000 x 9/12 =	£21,000		
01.01.93 to 05.04.93 £32,000 x 3/12 =	£8,000		
		£29,000	£20,000

	1993/94		
06.04.93 to 31.12.93 £32,000 x 9/12 =	£24,000		
01.01.94 to 05.04.94 £27,000 x 3/9 =	£9,000		
		£33,000	£28,000
		£62,000	£48,000

INCOME FROM PENSIONS YEAR TO 5.04.1995

STATE PENSION

Retirement or the old person's pensions are taxable, but the Department of Social Security do not operate PAYE when you receive it. If your state pension is your only source of income generally, no tax is payable, as your personal allowances will be greater than your income.

If your taxable state benefits are greater than your tax-free allowances and you are taxed under PAYE, your other earnings or pension will have to be taxed at a higher-than-normal rate, e.g. at 30% rather than 25%, to collect the extra tax on your state benefits. Your tax code will then include the letter F or K after 5th April 1994.

From the 6th April 1990, a married woman is taxable on any state retirement pension she receives, even if it is payable on the strength of her husband's contributions. So just enter the amount payable to you.

OTHER PENSIONS

Unfortunately, these pensions are generally taxed under PAYE. So if you have a pension income from a former employer or any other source, you enter the details here.

Pensions from abroad are generally taxed on a preceding year basis, so your 1994/95 tax bill will be based on the pension you got from abroad during the tax year 1993/94. Remember, you may be able to claim credit for any foreign tax deducted from a foreign pension and certain war widow's pensions are tax-free.

Surpluses repaid from an FSAVC Scheme

Enter the amount of any repayment from an FSAVC Scheme (see page 182), give the gross amount as shown on the certificate you receive from the plan's administrator.

INCOME FROM PENSIONS YEAR TO 5.04.1996

If you were 60 years of age after the 5th April 1995 or will begin to receive a pension in this tax year, you should complete this section, as it enables your tax inspector to adjust your tax code.

The state pension age is 65 for a man and 60 for a woman. Remember, the Department of Social Security does not operate the PAYE system and state pensions are paid gross. This does not really matter if you have no other source of income, as your personal allowance will normally be greater than your state pension. However, if you have additional income to the State pension, you will need to have your tax code adjusted to take account of this; otherwise, you could end up owing tax at the end of the tax year.

INCOME FROM NATIONAL INSURANCE AND SOCIAL SECURITY BENEFITS - YEAR TO 5.04.1995

Complete this section if, in the 1994/95 tax year you received:
- unemployment benefit
- income support (because you were unemployed, on short-time work, temporarily laid off or on strike)
- invalid care allowance
- widowed mother's allowance
- industrial death benefit (other than a lump sum)
- sick pay or maternity pay paid by the DSS
- invalidity allowance when paid with retirement pension
- job release allowance
- old person's pension
- retirement pension
- widow's pension

All other DSS benefits are tax-free.

INCOME FROM PROPERTY

FURNISHED ROOMS IN YOUR ONLY OR MAIN RESIDENCE

If you are an owner-occupier or a tenant and you let furnished accommodation in your only main residence, you may be entitled to "Rent a Room" relief.

With this relief you can receive a gross rent of up to £3,250 in the tax year without incuring a tax liability. If, however, your gross rental income exceeds £3,250 in the tax year you have an option of either paying tax on the excess, without relief for any expenses incurred, or paying tax on the nett rent received as outlined later.

Example:

Paul rents a room in his house in 1994/95. His gross income is £4,500 and he has allowable expenses of £1,250 and he pays tax at 25%. His position is as follows:

	With Rent a Room Relief	Taxed in the normal manner
Gross Rent	£4,500	£4,500
Less Expenses	-	£1,250
	£4,500	£3,250
"Rent a Room Relief"	£3,250	-
Taxable	£1,250	£3,250
Tax @ 25%	£313	£813

If you wish to claim this relief you must inform your tax inspector within one year of the end of the relevant tax year.

The tax free amount of £3,250 will be reduced to £1,625 if more than one person is letting a furnished room in your home.

Other Rental Income in UK

Nowadays, all income is taxed at the same rate. However, what Schedule or even what Case within a Schedule, you are taxed under is still important, as different rules apply under each Schedule. For example, a Schedule may determine what date your tax liability falls due and what expenses or expenditure you are entitled to offset against the income before your tax liability is calculated.

Rental income can be taxed under the following headings:

Schedule A	Unfurnished Lettings.
Schedule D Case I	Lettings carried out in the nature of a trade, such as hotels and tied public houses. Furnished holiday accommodation run on a commercial basis.
Schedule D Case VI	Furnished lettings. Holiday accommodation or letting of furnished holiday accommodation not run on a commercial basis.
Schedule D Case V	Rental Income from abroad.

Note: From 6th April 1995 all rental income from property situated in the UK will be taxable under Schedule A.

From April 1990 income that you and your spouse receive from jointly-owned assets will need to be split. Your tax inspector will split this income equally, unless you have agreed to split it on a different basis, and make a joint declaration to the tax office setting out how you wish the property income shared. Declarations made before the 6th June 1990, can apply to income arising before that date, however, declarations made after 6th June 1990 are only effective from the date of the declaration.

On your tax return, you enter the address of any property or land you own and the full amount of rents which you are entitled to receive. Only the net rental income (i.e. gross rent less expenses) is taxable, so it would be a good idea to enclose a statement showing how you arrive at the taxable amount for each property.

RENTAL STATEMENT

NAME _____   TAX NO.   _____
                                  Y/E   _____

Rents Receivable   _____
Community Charge   _____
Insurance on Premises   _____
Repairs and Renewals   _____
Light, Heat and Telephone   _____
Cleaning and Maintenance   _____
Agency and Advertising Charges _____
Interest on Borrowed Money   _____   _____
Sundry Expenses   _____   _____
SURPLUS

Furnished Holiday Letting

If lettings are carried on in the nature of a trade, they are assessable under Schedule D Case I. The letting of a home will be considered a business and taxed under Schedule D Case I if:

- it is a guest house.
- it is furnished holiday accommodation in the UK.

161

Letting of holiday accommodation may be treated as being 'on a commercial basis' and taxable under this heading if:

- you charge separately for cleaning and laundry services etc. The income received from these services will count as business income. However, the rent from the rooms may be taxed under Sch. D Case VI.

- it is available for letting for at least 140 days during each 12 month qualifying period and is actually let for 70 of these days during the 12 month period.

- it is not occupied continuously for more than 32 days by the same tenant during 7 of the 12 months.

- you pay somebody to provide services in furnished accommodation.

An advantage of Schedule D Case I assessment is that rental profits are considered as earned income and qualify for allowances such as capital allowances. Losses can be carried forward or offset against other earned income such as PAYE income and trading profits. The income can also be taken into account for a personal pension plan. Capital gains tax, roll-over and retirement relief are also available.

A rental statement, setting out income or expenses under separate headings, would simplify your tax computations. Also, ensure that you keep details of all expenses, especially for repairs and maintenance, as your inspector may wish to examine these.

Furnished Property

Unless you elect to be taxed under Schedule A, your income from furnished lettings is normally taxed under Schedule D Case IV. Furnished lettings include furnished holiday accommodation lettings, and are taxed on the actual profits for the year of assessment. Expenses deductible are similar to those under Schedule A. However, you can claim capital allowances on the cost of furniture replaced or you may claim an allowance for the cost of renewing furniture and equipment. This allowance is usually set at about 10% of your rental income less any rates or service charges you pay.

Tax on rental income for the year ending in the tax year 1994/95 is payable on the 1st January 1995 and subject to adjustment after the 5th April 1995.

Losses can be carried forward and offset against future profits or offset against other Schedule D Case VI income.

UNFURNISHED PROPERTY

Rents received, less expenses incurred during the letting period, are taxed on an actual basis and tax is due on the 1st January each year within the tax year, e.g. 1995/96 demand is payable on 1st January 1996.

Deductible expenses are:-

Maintenance and repair of the property, services provided, insurances, water rates, rent payable, capital allowances on equipment provided and management expenses. If your spouse takes part in the management of the property you should consider paying a salary. Capital expenses, such as the cost of extensions and improvements to the premises, are not deductible.

However, rental losses may be carried forward and offset against future Schedule A profits.

Ground rents or feu duties

Give details of UK ground rents or feu duties received and other income from property where the only expense is the cost of collection.

Land

Enter its location and the full amount of the rent due for the year, the expenses paid and net income. Enclose a statement outlining expenses.

Rental Premium

If you receive a premium from a tenant who has been given a lease of 50 years or less, a proportion of this premium is deemed to be rental income and is taxed accordingly. The formula for calculating the rental income element is:

$$A - \frac{A \times (B - 1)}{50}$$

Where A = Premium
       B = Number of years of lease

Example:

You grant a lease of 21 years to your tenant for a rental premium of £10,000. The amount to be added to your rental income is as follows:

$$£10,000 - \frac{(10,000 \times 20)}{50} = £6,000$$

Rental premiums are also deemed to be received; if a tenant agrees to carry out improvements to a property or surrenders a lease for money's worth.

Property Abroad:

If you have rental income from property outside the UK you may be liable to tax on this income even if it is not brought back into the UK. If, however, you have paid foreign tax on any foreign rents you may be allowed to deduct this tax from any UK tax due. Income from land and property abroad is normally tax under Schedule D Case V.

INCOME FROM SAVINGS & INVESTMENTS YEAR TO 5.04.1995

If you have savings and investments held in joint names, you should enter only your share of the income. Normally you should split the income equally. If you are married you can elect to declare the interest in unequal shares if you actually own the asset in unequal shares. This election cannot be back-dated. If you are in partnership enter your share of the partnership investment income.

Income from savings and investments are normally taxed on a previous year basis, i.e. your tax liability for 1994/95 is based on the interest paid or credited in the 1993/94 tax year.

National Savings Bank Ordinary Account

Interest is calculated on your lowest balance in your account for each calendar month and is credited to your account at 31st December each year.

Interest is paid gross and is taxable. However, your first £70 interest on an ordinary account is exempt from tax.

National Savings Bank Investment Account Interest

Interest is paid gross from the date when funds are deposited until the day prior to withdrawal. Interest is also credited to your account at 31st December each year and there is no exemption from tax.

Deposit Bonds & Income Bonds

Enter the details as shown on the relevant statement.

Capital Bonds

Interest is not paid on Capital Bonds until the end of the five year term. However, interest earned is taxed annually.

INCOME FROM OTHER UK BANKS, BUILDING SOCIETIES AND DEPOSIT TAKERS

Enter the name of your Bank, Building Society or any deposit held in the UK where tax has been deducted. The interest you receive is treated as having suffered basic-rate tax (25%) and you will not have to pay any more tax if you are a basic-rate taxpayer only. A 20% tax payer can claim a refund totaling 5% of gross interest earned, higher-rate taxpayers will pay additional tax on this interest, at the difference between the basic rate and the higher rate.

Example:

Eric has £1,000 in a Building Society, and is a higher-rate taxpayer. In 1994/95 he received £75 interest. Eric's tax position is as follows: As he has already suffered tax at the basic rate, his grossed-up interest is:

Gross Interest	£100
Tax Liability @ 40%	£40
Basic Rate Tax Already Paid	£25
Additional Tax Liability	£15

Do not include interest and terminal bonuses paid by a contractual savings scheme run by a Building Society, as they are not taxable.

Remember to enter the interest from a Personal Equity Plan which is paid directly to you, instead of being reinvested by the Plan Manager, if the gross amount paid exceeds £180.

Other Interest you receive in the UK

Here, you enter interest received on Certificates of Tax Deposit and interest on British Government Stocks (Gilts) available through the National Savings Stock Register and interest from credit unions and friendly societies.

You do not need to enter any non-taxable interest:

- Interest on National Savings Certificates.
- Ulster Savings Certificates (if the holder is resident and ordinarily resident in Northern Ireland).
- Interest awarded by a UK court as part of an award of damages for personal injury.
- Interest, dividends and bonuses arising on a Tax Exempt Special Savings Account (TESSA).
- Interest and terminal bonuses under the SAYE scheme.
- Gross interest not exceeding £180 withdrawn from a Personal Equity Plan (PEP).

DIVIDENDS FROM SHARES IN UK COMPANIES

Give the name of each shareholding and state the amount of the dividend and its tax credit. Also include any income from Unit Trusts, if the voucher shows a tax credit, even if it is reinvested in further units. Dividends are taxed on a current year basis, i.e. your tax liability for the 1994/95 tax year is based on income received in that year.

Example:

Andrew received a dividend of £240 in the tax year 1994/95. The voucher shows a dividend of £240 and a tax credit of £60. Andrew is a higher-rate taxpayer. His extra income tax liability is as follows:

Dividend	£240
Tax Credit	£60
Total Investment Income	£300
Tax @ 40%	£120
Less Tax Credit	£60
Extra Tax Payable	£60

From 6th April 1994, tax credits on dividends paid by UK companies are reduced from 25% to 20%. Basic and low rate taxpayers will pay no more tax on these dividends. However, higher rate taxpayers will be liable to pay additional tax charge at 20%, i.e. the difference between the higher rate tax and the tax credit.

STOCK DIVIDENDS

Stock dividends are dividends takens by way of additional stocks or shares rather than in cash. So this section includes taxable dividend income which you may have received by exercising a stock dividend option. These options will be treated for tax purposes as if you have received the dividend in cash. If, however, the cash equivalent is substantially less than the normal market value of the shares, on the day market dealings commence, your inspector may substitute that market value for the cash value.

INCOME FROM UK UNIT TRUSTS

On your tax return enter the amount of the distribution and the amount of the tax credit.

The first distribution you get from a Unit Trust is usually an equalisation payment and it is non-taxable.

With an accumulation unit trust the amount reinvested apart from any equalisation payment is income for tax purposes and is taxable.

If you buy unit trusts within a Personal Equity Plan, the income will be tax-free.

ACCRUED INCOME, CHARGES AND ALLOWANCES

Interest payments are made on Government gilts twice a year. You are entitled to receive the interest payments if you hold the security on a specified date. If a stock is sold after this date, it is sold "ex div", a stock sold before this date is sold "cum div".

Accrued interest is subject to income tax, unless the total nominal value of all the stocks you hold is £5,000 or less.

Your contract note will show the amount of accrued interest involved in each transaction and this accrued interest is taxed as follows:

- If you sell cum-dividend, you are taxed on the accrued interest included in the price you get.
- If you sell ex-dividend, you get tax relief on the accrued interest that has been deducted from the quoted price.
- If you buy cum-dividend, you get tax relief on the accrued interest included in the price you pay.
- If you buy ex-dividend, you are taxed on the accrued interest which has been deducted from the price paid.

For more details about the way accrued interest is taxed, see Inland Revenue leaflet IR68.

INCOME FROM SAVINGS AND INVESTMENT ABROAD

This includes overseas dividends, interest etc. Enter the full amount arising in the year to the 5th April 1995, whether or not you have received it in the UK. You can deduct expenses which arise abroad in managing and collecting this income. Also include details of overseas tax paid and UK tax deducted if any.

Example:

In 1994/95 Eric a higher rate tax payer received a foreign dividend of £1,500 with a £150 foreign tax already deducted. His tax position will work out as follows:

Gross Dividend		£1,500
Foreign Tax Deducted	£150	
Additional Tax Payable		
(£1,500 @ 40% less £150 already paid)	£450	
Total Tax		£600
Net Dividend		£900

NOTE: When foreign income is paid through an agent in the UK, basic rate tax will normally be accounted for by the agent after allowing for any relevant double taxation agreement between the UK and the foreign country. Basic rate taxpayers will not be liable to any more tax, however, higher rate taxpayers will pay additional tax at the difference between basic rate and higher rate tax. When foreign income is paid to you directly from abroad you may have to apply for any relevant double taxation relief yourself to Inspector of Foreign Dividends, Lynwood Road, Thames Ditton, Surrey KT7 ODP.

OTHER INCOME FROM SAVINGS & INVESTMENTS

ANNUITIES

With an annuity, you purchase from an insurance company a guaranteed income for a specifice period or for the rest of your life.

Part of your income from an annuity is capital and tax free, the remainder is interest and taxable.

An insurance company will normally deduct tax at the basic rate from the taxable part of an annuity. If you are liable for less tax than the insurance company deducts you can claim it back. If your taxable income from all sources is equal to or less than your age-related allowances you may apply to have your annuity income paid gross by completing form R89.

LIFE ASSURANCE

Gains on life assurance policies, life annuity contracts and capital redemption policies are not normally taxed, if such contracts are qualifying life assurance contracts or if they commenced on or before the 19th March 1968.

Qualifying Life Assurance Contracts

A qualifying policy must be certified as such by the Inland Revenue. It is generally one where the premium is paid regularly at least once a year over a period of 10 or more years and has a minimum guaranteed-sum-assured payable on death.

The proceeds from qualifying policies are tax-free, assuming they were in force for the required minimum term.

Non-Qualifying Life Assurance Contracts

Up to 5% of the premium or premiums paid may be withdrawn annually tax-free from a non-qualifying life assurance contract. However, other gains from a non-qualifying policy may be subject to some tax on death, maturity, sale or encashment.

The taxable gain on termination of a policy is the excess of the cash value after account has been taken of previous withdrawals and premiums paid. The gain when it arises, is added to your taxable income. If you were and remain a basic-rate taxpayer after the gain is added to your income, no additional tax is payable. If you were a basic-rate taxpayer before this gain was added to your income but a higher-rate taxpayer after the gain was added to your income, you may claim top-slicing relief.

Under top-slicing relief, the average yearly gain since the policy commenced is added to your income. If, after this average gain is added to your income, you still remain a basic-rate taxpayer, no extra tax is payable. However, if this average yearly gain pushed you into the higher tax bracket, the average rate of tax payable on the gain is calculated and this new rate, less basic-rate tax, is applied to your overall gain.

Example:

You purchased a bond for £10,000 five years ago and you encashed it in March 1995 for £16,000. Your gain is £6,000. Your taxable income in 1994/95 is £23,000. Additional tax on the gain is calculated as follows:

| Gain ÷ years held | £6,000 ÷ 5 | £1,200 |
| Taxable income plus average gain | | £24,200 |

Tax Payable on Average Gain

Amount of Gain	Tax Rate	Tax
£700	25%	£175
£500	40%	£200
£1,200		£375

Average Tax Rate

375 ÷ 1,200 X 100   =   31.25

Rate Applied to overall gain is 6.25% or   (31.25% - 25%)

The tax payable on £6,000 gain is   £6,000 X 6.25% = £375

If you were a higher-rate taxpayer before this gain was added to your income you pay additional tax on the taxable gain at 15% i.e. the difference between the basic-rate and the higher rate tax.

Remember, Life Assurance Offices are required to inform the Inland Revenue of any chargeable gain arising on non-qualifying policies.

OTHER INCOME YEAR TO 5.04.1995

Income from Trusts funded by others

A trust is a legal entity set up under a deed to take charge of, or to manage, assets for the benefit of named beneficiaries.

A settlement is the legal term for creating a trust under a Deed or a Will.

A trust pays tax on their income at the basic rate, unless it is a discretionary trusts. If as a beneficiary, you receive income from a trust, it will be paid with basic-rate tax already deducted. If you are a non-taxpayer you can reclaim this tax. If you are a higher-rate taxpayer, you will pay the additional tax in the normal way.

Discretionary Trusts

The rate of tax paid on discretionary trust income is the basic rate plus an additional rate. For 1994/95, this additional rate is 10%.

INCOME & CAPITAL FROM SETTLEMENTS FOR WHICH YOU HAVE PROVIDED FUNDS

Income and gains from a settlement for which you have directly or indirectly provided funds will normally be treated as yours for tax purposes and should be entered here.

Accumulation and Maintenance Trusts

This is a special type of trust which is commonly set up for young children.

The income earned or guaranteed can be accumulated or used for the children's maintenance, education etc. Normally, the trust comes to an end and the remaining property is distributed some time after the children reach 18.

If income is accumulated until your children reach 18 it may not be taxed as your own personal income.

Tax is normally deducted by the trustees at the basic rate plus 10%, making a total of 35%. If you are liable at the basic rate only, you can reclaim this 10% from the Inland Revenue and repay it to the trustees or to your children.

INCOME FROM ESTATES

You should enter the name of the deceased person, the date of death and the name and address of the executor or personal representative administering the estate. You should also state the type of interest you have in the estate. e.g. absolute interest or life interest. Usually, a personal representative will give you an income tax certificate (R185), showing your gross income from the date of death.

MAINTENANCE AND ALIMONY YOU RECEIVE

Whether you pay tax on any maintenance you get depends on whether it is voluntary or enforceable and the date the agreement was made.

If you receive voluntary maintenance payments you do not have to pay tax on what you get.

If you receive enforceable maintenance under a court order or other legally binding agreement the following rules apply:

- If the agreement was made after 14th March 1988 (or if it was applied for before then but was not in place by 30th June 1988), what you receive is treated as tax-free income.
- If the agreement was made before 15th March 1988 (or it was applied for before that date and was in place by 30th June 1988) you will not pay tax on the first £1,720 of maintenance you receive in the 1994/95 tax year. Anything over this amount will count as taxable income. But the taxable amount of maintenance is "pegged" to the amount on which you paid tax in the 1988/89 tax year. If the amount of maintenance you get increased after 5th April 1989 you will not have to pay tax on the extra you receive.
- If the agreement was made before 15th March 1988 and you are a child receiving maintenance from a parent or step-parent the amount that counts for tax is "pegged" to the amount that was taxable in the 1988/89 tax year. Any increases since then are not taxable.

MAINTENANCE FROM A FORMER PARTNER
If you receive maintenance from a former partner to whom you were never married, this income is tax free whether the agreements are enforceable or voluntary.

PERSONAL ALLOWANCES

In the tax year in which you part, you will get the following allowances:
- a husband will get his own personal allowance plus the full married couple's allowance.
- a wife will get her own personal allowance plus the additional personal allowance if she has at least one child living with her.

In following tax years, both ex-partners will get their own personal allowance plus any other allowances they are entitled to, e.g. additional personal allowance. A husband can continue to claim the married couple's allowance if all the following apply:
- he is still married, i.e. is separated but not divorced
- since the separation he has wholly maintained his wife by making voluntary maintenance payments.
- he is not claiming an additional personal allowance.-

ALL OTHER INCOME OR PROFITS

This section is a 'sweeping up' section designed to include any other income which does not easily fit into any of the foregoing sections.

MORTGAGE OR LOAN FOR MAIN HOME

Interest payments may be subdivided into two major categories:
- Qualifying Home Loans
- Other Loans

Qualifying Home

A qualifying home is normally your sole or main residence and must be situated in the UK or the Republic of Ireland. It may be freehold or leasehold. A caravan or mobile home can also qualify, provided it is more than 22 feet long and 7.5 feet wide. A home boat could also qualify, provided it has been designed, or adapted, as a home.

Relief may also be available if you normally live in accommodation provided by your employer and you are purchasing a property which you occassionaly live in or intend to live in as your main home.

Qualifying Interest

The amount of interest qualifying for tax relief at the lower rate (20%) in 1994/95 under a home loan is normally the interest charged on all or part of the first £30,000 of the loan. From the 6th April 1995 the rate of tax relief is reduced to 15%. Other factors may also be relevant for tax relief purposes, such as the date and the purpose for which the loans were taken out.

LOANS MADE OUT ON OR BEFORE THE 6th APRIL 1988

Interest on qualifying loans before the 6th April 1988, is allowed as a tax-deduction, provided the purpose of the loan was to buy or improve a sole or main residence for:-
- yourself
- your divorced or separated spouse, whether the residence is owned by you alone or jointly
- your widowed, divorced or separated mother or mother-in-law or any other relative who cannot work because of old age, permanent illness or disablement and who occupies the residence without any form of payment.

Interest paid on these loans continues to qualify for relief provided the property has been used as the main home of the same person since before 6th April 1988.

LOANS MADE OUT ON OR AFTER THE 6th APRIL 1988

Interest on a qualifying loan after the 5th April 1988, is allowed as a tax deduction, provided the purpose of the loan was to purchase a sole or main residence for yourself or your spouse.

If you take out a home loan for any of the following purposes after the 5th April 1988, it will not qualify for tax relief:

- Home improvements or loans taken out to replace an earlier home improvement loan. If part of the replacement loan is for house purchase and part for home improvements, only the house purchase part of the replacement loan is allowable.
- Loans to purchase a sole or main residence for your divorced or separated spouse, whether the residence is owned by you or jointly or any other relative who is unable to work because of old age or permanent illness or disablement.

Married Couples

Up to the 5th April 1990, relief for interest paid was normally given to the husband, unless the wife had elected for separate assessment.

From the 6th April 1990, if the loan is in one name only, tax relief will be given to the named spouse. If the loan is in joint names, relief will be split equally, unless you complete Form 15 whereby you can elect to share this relief in any way you choose. This form must be signed by both spouses and submitted to your tax office within 12 months of the end of the relevant tax year.

Electing for an interest split other than on a 50/50 basis may be beneficial if:

- only one spouse is liable to pay tax
- one spouse is 65 or older and has income above the income limit for the higher allowance.

If you wish to make an election for 1995/96 and have not submitted Form 15, you should tick the appropriate space. Your Tax Office will send you a form to enable you make an election.

YEAR OF MARRIAGE

If you or your spouse each had a mortgage which qualified for tax relief before you married and you were not living together, and you now intend to sell both homes you can:

- continue to get the tax relief on the old homes for up to twelve months and
- jointly get tax relief on loans up to £30,000 to buy your new home.

Alternatively, if you decide to live in one of your existing homes you can:

- continue to get tax relief on the home you are selling for up to 12 months and
- continue to get tax relief, as before on the home in which you live.

If you were living together before you married and qualified for mortgage interest relief on up to £60,000 on a joint mortgage you will only get tax relief on the amount of loan up to £30,000 from the date you get married.

SEPARATION / DIVORCE

If you are getting a separation or a divorce and you need to raise money to buy your spouse's share of your existing home, this loan may qualify for tax relief within the normal limits.

Even if the home is in one name only, the other spouse may have a legal interest in the home, e.g. the right to occupy it, and this legal right may be purchased with a qualifying home loan.

Loans before the 1st August 1988

Before the 1st August 1988, a single person or a married couple could qualify for tax relief on interest paid on a qualifying home loan up to £30,000. Two single people jointly buying a home before the 1st August 1988 could claim mortgage interest relief on a £60,000 mortgage. This is now no longer possible, as interest relief on all new loans after the 1st August 1988 is applicable to the home and not the purchaser(s).

However, if you took out a mortgage for more than £30,000 as one of two single people before the 1st August 1988, the full amount of this mortgage may still qualify for tax relief as long as the mortgage remains in force and you do not marry.

In the event of remortgage, the mortgage-interest will be limited to interest on the first £30,000, even if the new mortgage is taken out by the same two people.

Bridging Loans

If you have to take out a bridging loan on a new home before you have sold your existing home, the mortgage on your old home is excluded when calculating the amount of tax relief relevant to your new home. So in effect, you may claim tax relief on both loans. This concession is for a period of 12 months, or longer in deserving cases.

Claiming Relief

If you have a building society mortgage, enter the name of the society and your account number and tick the box if the interest is not paid through the MIRAS system. With all other qualifying home loans, enter the name of the lender, the account number and the amount of interest paid in the tax year. If your loan is outside the MIRAS system include a certificate of interest paid.

OTHER QUALIFYING LOANS

Enclose a certificate of interest paid and enter the name of the lender and the amount of interest. Loans which would qualify for relief include:

- Loans to buy ordinary shares in or lend money to a close company which you manage or own more than 5% of its ordinary share capital. From 14th March 1989, this interest will not qualify for relief if the shares qualify for tax relief under the Business Expansion Scheme.
- Loans to buy an interest in or to provide capital to a partnership.
- Loans of less than £30,000 to purchase an annuity if you are 65 or older and if the loan is secured on your main residence in the UK or the Republic of Ireland. This type of loan attracts tax relief at 25%.
- Loans to buy plant and machinery used by your partnership or business.

Normally, interest on loans to buy or improve property in the UK may be offset against the rental income, provided the property was:

- let for more than 26 weeks at a full commercial rent
- available for letting for the rest of the 52 week period.

Enter the number of weeks for which the property was let and the interest paid. From April 1990, where you and your wife own the property, interest payable on joint loans will be split equally between you, unless you give details showing that you and your spouse contribute in unequal amounts towards the interest payments.

PENSION CONTRIBUTIONS

Personal Pensions

If your employer does not operate a group pension scheme or if you are self-employed, you can set up a personal pension plan.

Basically, personal pension plans are savings plans designed to give you an income on retirement and to give financial protection in the event of your premature death or disability.

They are particularly attractive because up to certain limits, contributions are fully tax-deductible.

Tax Relief

The percentage of your net relevant earnings qualifying for tax relief depends on your age and the plan type.

Net Relevant Earnings

If you are an employee, your net relevant earnings are generally your gross earnings plus taxable fringe-benefits, less allowable expenses. If you are self-employed, your net relevant earnings will normally mean taxable profits, less capital allowances, stock relief and any losses from earlier years which have not been offset against other income.

In the 1989/90 tax year, a cap of £60,000 was placed on net relevant earnings qualifying for pension tax relief. This earnings cap will be increased each year in line with the retail price index. For the tax years 1992/93 and 1993/94 the capped figure is £75,000. For 1994/95 the figure is £76,800.

Plan Type

Your plan type was determined when you commenced contributions. If yours commenced before the 1st July 1988 it is the 'old-type' plan. If you commenced contributions on or after the 1st July 1988 it is a 'new-type' plan.

The following percentages of net relevant earnings qualify for tax relief under each:

Age on 6th April	Old-Type Plan	New-Type Plan
35 or Under	17.5%	17.5%
36 to 45	17.5%	20.0%
46 to 50	17.5%	25.0%
51 to 55	20.0%	30.0%
56 to 60	22.5%	35.0%
61 to 74	27.5%	40.0%
Over 74	NIL	NIL

Maximum Contributions

The rules are complicated and depend to some extent on how much you have already contributed. If you pay too much into an old-style plan, you will not get tax relief on the excess. If you pay too much into one of the new-type personal pension plans, your excess contributions will be refunded.

Carry-Back Rules

The carry-back rules allow you to claim tax relief in a previous year, provided the premium was paid in the current tax year and you have enough unused tax relief in that year to cover the amount carried-back. If you had no net relevant earnings in the previous year, you can carry-back the contribution two years and get tax relief at your highest rate applicable in that year.

Example:

In 1994/95 you make a contribution of £8,000 to a personal pension plan, your position was as follows:

Tax Year	Net Relevant Earnings	Contr. Entitlement 17.5%	Already Paid	Contr. available to be carried back	Contr. Carried Back
1994/95	£35,000	£6,125	£8,000	£1,875	
1993/94	£32,000	£5,600	£3,000		£1,875

Carry-Forward Rules

If you have not made the maximum pension contributions over the past six years, you may now make additional contributions to take advantage of these reliefs by way of the carry-forward rules.

Example:

Assuming your position is as follows:

Tax Year	Net Relevant Earnings	Contributions Entitlements	Paid	Possible Additional Contributions
1994/95	£33,000	£5,775	£1,000	£4,775
1993/94	£27,000	£4,725	£1,000	£3,725
1992/93	£29,000	£5,075	£1,000	£4,075
1991/92	£21,000	£3,675	£1,000	£2,675
1990/91	£13,000	£2,275	£1,000	£1,275
1989/90	£11,000	£1,925	-	£1,925
1988/89	£9,000	£1,575	-	£1,575
Total				£20,025

Deduct your Current Year Relief	£4,775
Pension Contributions for back-years	
qualifying for full tax relief	£15,250

Suppose you now wish to pay say, £12,000, in addition to your regular commitment of £1,000 p.a.:

The current year's maximum must be paid in full before the carry-forward provisions operate. The maximum contribution in the current year is £5,775, of which £1,000 has already been paid. So £7,225 is available to offset against previous years' unused pension relief i.e. £12,000 less £4,775.

This £7,225 is first offset against your earliest available year's unused relief, and then the balance is offset against unused relief in the following years until your overall contribution is used up. So your position will work out as follows:

The 1988/89 Allowance	£1,575
- The 1989/90 Allowance	£1,925
- The 1990/91 Allowance	£1,275
- Part of the 1991/92 Allowance	£2,450
	£7,225

Generally, your tax inspector will automatically apportion your excess contributions in this way, so you should have no need to outline the details. However, if you wish to make the allocation yourself, you may normally do so before the 5th July immediately following the end of the tax year in which the additional payment was made:

- Form PP43 - for Personal Pension Plan
- Form 43 - for Retirement Annuities.

Employees

Employees get basic-rate relief at source on contributions paid to an approved personal pension plan. If you are a higher-rate taxpayer, you may claim the higher relief through your tax code or by rebate at the end of the tax year.

Self-Employed

If you are self-employed, you do not get tax relief at source. It is given by means of an allowance in your Schedule D assessment.

FSAVC

If you are already in an employer's pension scheme, you may make additional contributions to top-up your benefits at retirement and give yourself a better pension.

This mechanism is usually referred to as Additional Voluntary Contributions or AVC.

However, if you want to set up an AVC plan totally-independently of your employer's pension scheme, you can do so by way of Free-Standing Additional Voluntary Contributions - FSAVC.

Your FSAVC benefits are aggregated with all other pension benefits in determining the maximum benefits permitted by the Inland Revenue. You may not contribute to more than one FSAVC plan in any one tax year in respect of the same employment. So you can have the choice of an AVC scheme arranged in conjunction with the company's scheme, or a FSAVC plan arranged with a recognised pension provider. With a FSAVC plan you may have a wider choice of investment media and more flexible modes of payment. However, your employer's scheme may be more cost-effective, with lower administrations costs, as many employers include the administration costs of AVC plans under the main scheme. Under a FSAVC plan, you pay the administration costs yourself.

TAX

Tax relief is available on contributions paid to a FSAVC or an AVC plan up to a maximum of 15% of your net relevant earnings. This 15% also includes any contributions you already pay to your employers main pension scheme.

Trade Union or Friendly Society Death Benefit and Superannuation Schemes

You can get tax relief on premiums which you pay on certain combined sickness and life insurance policies offered by Friendly Societies. The tax relief is at half your top rate of tax on the life part of the premium. You can also get the same tax relief on part of your trade union subscription if it includes superannuation, funeral or life insurance benefits.

Friendly Societies also offer investment-type life insurance policies which can offer a tax-free return in the same way as normal life insurance policies. However, there are strict limits on the size of the policies which qualify for this tax relief. The limit for 1994/95 is £200 and £270 after the 1995/96 tax year.

Also, include here compulsory payments to provide annuities for widows and orphans, where relief is not given automatically by your employer.

Death, Sickness and Superannuation Benefits

Do not claim relief on payments if tax relief on contributions for death, sickness and superannuation benefits has already been given by the Assurance Company or Friendly Society, either by reducing the premiums or increasing the benefits. Also, relief should not be claimed where your employer deducts the amount of your allowable-contribution from your earnings before operating PAYE.

OTHER DEDUCTIONS

MAINTENANCE OR ALIMONY PAYMENTS

There are two types of maintenance payments:

- Enforceable payments
- Voluntary Payments

You do not get tax relief on voluntary maintenance payment you make.

If you make enforceable maintenance payments, the rules on tax relief vary depending on whom the maintenance payments are paid to and when the legally binding agreement was made. Certain payments will not qualify for tax relief:

- payments for which you already get tax relief in some other way e.g. mortgage interest.
- payments under a foreign court order or agreement.
- capital payments or lump sums, even if they are paid in instalments.

AGREEMENTS MADE AFTER 15TH MARCH 1988

Maintenance paid to your ex-spouse.

You get tax relief on enforceable payment up to the maintenance deduction limit of £1,720. In 1994/95 relief is given at 20% only on maintenance payments made up to a maximum of £1,720 (in 1995/96 relief will be restricted to 15%). All periodical payments and bill paid on behalf of your spouse count towards this limit if they are covered by a court order or other legally binding agreement. Tax relief stops if you ex-spouse remarries.

Maintenance paid to children.

You will not get tax relief if the payments are made direct to a child. However, if the wording of the court order say that the money is paid to your ex-spouse for the children, then tax relief is available within the above limits.

Maintenance paid to a Former Partner

If you are paying maintenance to a former partner to whom you were never married no tax relief is available whether they are enforceable or voluntary payments.

AGREEMENTS MADE BEFORE 15TH MARCH 1988 in place by 30th June 1988)

Maintenance paid to your ex-spouses.

The tax relief you can get on enforceable payments is limited to the amount of maintenance payments you paid which qualified for tax relief in the 1988/89 tax year. For example, if you paid £3,000 maintenance in the 1988/89 tax year, you'll get tax relief on no more than £3,000 of maintenance payments in future tax years. The only exception to this rule is where the court order provided for automatic increases in payments e.g. where the maintenance you pay is linked to the rate of inflation. In such circumstances you can get full tax relief on the payments you make.

Maintenance paid to children.

The tax relief you receive is limited to the amount of maintenance you paid which qualified for tax relief in 1988/89.

Maintenance paid to a Former Partner

If you are paying maintenance to a former partner to whom you were never married no tax relief is available whether they are enforceable or voluntary payments.

How to Make the Payments

Most enforceable maintenance payments should be paid in full, without deducting any tax. You will get tax relief through an adjustment in your PAYE code or it will be shown on your tax assessment.

The exception to this rule is payments dated before 15th March 1988 payable to children over 21. Here you deduct basic-rate tax and pay over the net amount. (Higher-rate tax relief will be given through an adjustment in your PAYE code of your tax assessment).

Allowances

In the tax year in which you part, you will get the following allowances:

- a husband will get his own personal allowance plus the full married couple's allowance.
- a wife will get her own personal allowance plus the additional personal allowance if she has at least one child living with her.

In the following tax years, both ex-partners will get their own personal allowance plus any other allowances they are entitled to e.g. additional personal allowance. A husband can continue to claim the married couple's allowance if all the following apply:

- he is still married, i.e. is separated but not divorced.
- since the separation he has wholly maintained his wife by making voluntary maintenance payments.
- he is not claiming an additional personal allowance.

PRIVATE MEDICAL INSURANCE FOR PEOPLE AGED 60 OR OVER

From the 6th April 1990, tax relief is available on premiums paid for private medical insurance policies for people aged 60 and over. This applies only if the policy does not pay a cash benefit should you opt to be treated under the National Health Service instead of being treated privately.

Non-taxpayers can also benefit from this relief, as basic-rate tax is deducted from the premiums at source and you only pay the net amount to the insurer.

In the 1994/95 tax year, if you pay private medical insurance premiums on behalf of someone else who is 60 or over, you may claim tax relief on the premiums. The relief is also available on joint policies between husbands and wives, even if only one spouse is 60 or over.

Relief is restricted to basic tax (25%) from 6th April 1994.

GIFT AID

Enter the net amount(s) and the name of the charity to which the payments were made. From the 1st October 1990, there is relief on gifts of cash to charities by individuals that are not made by way of covenant. The relief is due on gifts of amounts over £250 made on or after 16th March 1993 (£400 before 16th March 1993). The gift is made net of basic rate income tax and the donor qualifies for higher-rate relief as appropriate. The charity can claim repayment of the basic-rate tax deducted.

Covenants to Charity

Covenants are gratuitous payments under a deed, whereby you undertake to pay an annual or more frequent amount to another person or association.

Covenants to a charity qualify for tax relief, provided they are capable of lasting for more than three years.

Drawing up a Covenant

Charities usually have ready-made deeds of covenant for regular contributors. They usually specify that payments be made for a minimum period of four years.

The deed will contain the words 'signed, sealed and delivered'. It must be signed and dated before the first payment is made. A covenant cannot be backdated to include payments already made. The signing must be witnessed and the witness must also sign the deed. Although, in theory, the deed should be sealed by fixing a disc of paper, the Inland Revenue do not insist on this.

In Scotland, a deed does not have to be sealed and delivered or witnessed. Instead, you write the words 'Adopted as holograph' in you own handwriting above your signature and at the bottom of previous papers, if the deed covers more than one page.

When you complete a covenant to a charity, you deduct tax at the basic rate from the covenant amount and pay over the net balance to the charity.

After the first payment has been made the charity will send you an Inland Revenue Form R 185 AP to sign, showing the amount of your donation and the tax deducted. The charity needs this form to reclaim the tax deducted. If your covenant is for an amount less than £175 per year after deduction of tax, you need complete this form in year one only.

Enter on your tax return the net amount paid after deduction of basic rate tax.

Other Covenants, Bonds of Annuity and Settlements etc.

Covenants to individuals commenced after the 14th March 1988, do not qualify for tax relief. However, covenants existing before that date and on which you are already getting tax relief, continue to qualify for tax relief. Enter the *gross* amount in the case of covenants to individuals.

VOCATIONAL TRAINING

From 6th April 1992 tax relief is available for training which leads to a National Vocational Qualification or a Scottish Vocational Qualification up to and including level 5 (up to level 4 prior to 1st January 1994) regardless of when your training commenced.

Tax relief is available for the following:

- Study, examination and registration fees.
- Fees payable for assessment purposes including prior learning assessment.
- Payment for any award or certificate obtained.
- Payment for an entry in an official register such as the National Record of Achievement or the Record of Education and Training in Scotland.

However, no tax relief is available for payments made for equipment or textbooks or the cost of travelling or subsistence.

If you are eligible, you claim the basic relief by deducting basic rate tax from the fees you pay.

If you are a higher-rate taxpayer you claim the extra relief through your PAYE code.

NOTE   From January 1994 tax relief is no longer available to children under 16, or to 16 to 18 year olds at full time education or training which is mainly for recreation or leisure.

CAPITAL GAINS - 1994/95

Capital Gains Tax (CGT) is a tax on gains arising from the disposal of capital assets.

Persons Chargeable All persons resident in the UK for tax purposes are liable to the tax. Individuals who are resident and domiciled in the UK are chargeable on all gains wherever arising, while those who are resident and non-domiciled in the UK are liable only on non-UK gains to the extent that the gains are remitted to the UK.

Chargeable Assets All forms of property are assets for CGT purposes e.g. options, debts and foreign currencies, except those specifically exempted.

Disposal A disposal for CGT takes place whenever the ownership of an asset changes. This includes a part-disposal even where no payment is received e.g. a gift or exchange. An exception to this latter rule is on death. In the case of death, no chargeable disposal takes place and the person who receives the asset is treated as having acquired it at the market value at the date of the death.

EXEMPTIONS AND RELIEFS

Annual Allowance

The first £5,800 of chargeable gains arising to you in the 1994/95 tax year is exempt from capital gains tax (£6,000 in 1995/96).

If your total chargeable gains (before losses) are not more than £5,800 and the total proceeds from all disposals are not more than £11,600 all you normally need to do is enter "gains not exceeding £5,800 and disposals not exceeding £11,600".

Private Residence

Normally, no capital gains tax arises on the disposal of your sole or main private residence and grounds up to half a hectare in 1994/95 (one acre before 1991/92) provided it has been 'occupied' by you throughout the period of ownership.

However, capital gains which you are deemed to have made while you were living away from your sole or main home, may be liable to capital gains tax. For example, if you rented your home for five of the ten years you owned it, only half the gain would be exempt. There are exceptions to this rule, for example:

- If you cannot move into your new home within the first year because of alterations or because you could not sell your old home.
- Absences before the 31st March 1982.
- Certain periods during which you were away from your home because of your job are exempt.
- Normally, absences for any reason totalling up to three years, as long as you use the home as your sole or main residence for some time both before the first period of absence and after the last one.
- Any absences in the last three years before you sell your home are always exempt.

Other Assets

The following are normally exempt from capital gains tax:

- Private Cars
- National Savings Certificates, Premium Bonds, Capital Bonds and SAYE deposits.
- British money including post-1837 gold sovereigns.
- Currency for personal-use abroad.
- Betting winnings.
- British Government stocks and most corporate bonds, if acquired after the 13th March 1984.
- Shares, unit trusts and investment trusts held in a PEP.
- Shares issued after 18th March 1986 under the Business Expansion Scheme and which were sold more than five years after purchase.
- The proceeds from life insurance policies, provided you did not buy them from a third party.
- Damages for wrong or injury suffered in your private or professional life.
- Settled property.
- A gain on the disposal of an award for valour or gallant conduct.
- Gifts to charities or certain national institutions.
- A gift of heritage property, if certain conditions are satisfied.
- Any chattel which has a predictable useful life of no more than 50 years when you first acquired it, e.g. electronic equipment, yachts and race-horses, provided that you have not used the asset in your business so that it qualified for capital allowances.
- For chattels with a predictable life of more than 50 years, gains may be partly tax-free. Broadly speaking, if the disposal proceeds are less than £6,000, the gain is tax-free.

Married Couples

Before the 6th April 1990, a married couple got a £5,000 capital gains tax exemption. Following the introduction of independent taxation in April 1990, each spouse is now entitled to a separate annual exemption. This exemption in 1994/95 was £5,800. Transfers between spouses do not give rise to a capital gains tax charge - the spouse who receives an asset is deemed to have acquired it on the date and at the cost at which the other spouse acquired it, unless the parties are separated or divorced (except in the year of separation).

The capital losses of one spouse can no longer be offset against the gains of the other, including capital losses brought forward from the 6th April 1990.

Hold-Over Relief

Under hold-over relief, no CGT may be payable on gifts made before the 14th March 1989. After 14th March 1989, this relief is only available in respect of:

- business assets
- gifts which count as chargeable transfers for inheritance tax purposes (mainly gifts to companies and certain types of discretionary trusts).

By claiming hold-over relief, the gain is passed on to the recipient, who is in effect, taxed on the final disposal of the asset on the basis of the original market value.

Example;

In June 1990, Anne gave her sister Julia shares in XYZ Ltd. valued at £13,000, which she bought for £10,000 in January 1989. They claimed hold-over relief. In January 1994 Julia sold it for £19,000. Julia's gain (ignoring indexation) after claiming hold-over relief is £9,000 (£19,000 - £10,000 and not £19,000 - £13,000).

The donor and the UK-resident must claim the hold-over relief within six years of the gift being made.

Gifts made after the 14th March 1989

CGT may be paid in ten annual instalments, where the gift is land, controlling shareholding in a company or shareholdings in an unquoted company. Interest is charged on the unpaid tax.

Roll-over Relief

Tax may be deferred if the proceeds from the sale of business assets are reinvested in similar assets within 12 months before, or three years after, the sale. The assets which normally qualify are land, buildings, plant and machinery, ships, aircraft, hovercrafts and goodwill.

Retirement Relief

If you are aged 55 or more and retire, disposing of a business you owned for at least ten years before the 5th April 1995, you can receive a lump sum up to £250,000 (£150,000 before 5th April 1994) free of capital gains tax: half of the gain between £250,000 and £1,000,000 is taxable. For disposals made before 5th April 1994 half of the gain between £150,000 and £600,000 is taxable.

Chargeable Gains

Basically, the chargeable gain is calculated by deducting from the market value or proceeds received, the cost of the disposed asset plus allowable expenditure, indexation relief and your annual exemption.

Rates of Tax

You pay capital gains tax on the chargeable gain at your appropriate income tax rate.

Indexation Allowance

Before a taxable capital gain is calculated you are allowed adjust the base cost of the asset to take account of inflation.

For capital gains tax purposes Retail Price Indexation (RPI) began in 1982; gains before that date were not index linked. When working out your capital gains on an asset acquired before the 31st March 1982, you may elect to replace the asset base-cost by the market value at 31st March 1982, provided this election covers all assets you hold at 31st March 1982.

Indexation Factors

	Jan	Feb	Mar	Apr	May	Jun	Jul	Aug	Sep	Oct	Nov	Dec
1982	-	-	79.4	81.0	81.6	81.9	81.9	81.9	81.9	82.3	82.7	82.5
1983	82.6	83.0	83.1	84.3	84.6	84.8	85.3	85.7	86.1	86.4	86.7	86.9
1984	86.8	87.2	87.5	88.6	89.0	89.2	89.1	89.9	90.1	90.7	91.0	90.9
1985	91.2	91.9	92.8	94.8	95.2	95.4	95.2	95.5	95.4	95.6	95.9	96.0
1986	96.2	96.6	96.7	97.7	97.8	97.8	97.5	97.8	98.3	98.5	99.3	99.6
1987	100.0	100.4	100.6	101.8	101.9	101.9	101.8	102.1	102.1	102.9	103.4	103.3
1988	103.3	103.7	104.1	105.8	106.2	106.6	106.7	107.9	108.4	109.5	110.0	110.3
1989	111.0	111.8	112.3	114.3	115.0	115.4	115.5	115.8	116.6	117.5	118.5	118.8
1990	119.5	120.2	121.4	125.1	126.2	126.7	126.8	128.1	129.3	130.3	130.0	129.9
1991	130.2	130.9	131.4	133.1	133.5	134.1	133.8	134.1	134.6	135.1	135.6	135.7
1992	135.6	136.3	136.7	138.8	139.3	139.3	138.8	138.9	139.4	139.9	139.7	139.2
1993	137.9	138.8	139.3	140.6	141.1	141.0	140.7	141.3	141.9	141.8	141.6	141.9
1994	141.3	142.1	142.5	144.2	144.7	144.7	144.0	144.7	145.0	145.2	-	-

Indexation can only be used to reduce or extinguish a capital gain, after the 31st December 1993, indexation can not be used to covert a gain into a loss or increase a capital loss.

Example:

In May 1994, Eric sold a house for £125,000. Selling costs were £4,000. He bought the house in April 1981 for £31,000, including legal fees and stamp duty. Its market value at the 31st March 1982 was £48,000. He built an extension costing £10,000 in January 1990. The house was not his principal residence and he had no other chargeable gain in the tax year 1993/94. Eric paid basic-rate tax on £23,000 in 1994/95.

Sale Price		£125,000
Allowable Costs:		
Market Value at 31/03/82	£48,000	
Selling Costs	£4,000	
Extension	£10,000	£62,000
Un-indexed Gain		£63,000

Computation of Capital Gain 1994/95

The Indexation Allowance is calculated by multiplying the initial value and each allowable expense by the appropriate index factor.

Market Value 31.03.82   £48,000 X $\dfrac{144.70 - 79.4}{79.4}$ £39,476

Extension   £10,000 X $\dfrac{144.70 - 119.50}{119.50}$ £2,109

Total Indexation Allowance   £41,585

Un-indexed Gain	£63,000
Less Indexation Allowance	£41,585
Capital Gain	£21,415
Less Annual Exemption	£5,800
Subject to Capital Gains Tax	£15,615

Tax Payable:		
25%	£700	£175
40%	£14,915	£5,966
Capital Gains Tax Payable		£6,141

A trust is a legal entity set up under a deed to take charge of, or to manage, assets for the benefit of named beneficiaries.

A settlement is the legal term for creating a trust under a Deed or a Will.

If you are the settlor of a settlement

A trust is a legal entity set up under a deed to take charge of, or to manage, assets for the benefit of named beneficiaries. Before completing this section it is recommended you seek advice from your tax or financial advisor.

PAYMENTS ABROAD

Enter the gross amount of any payments you made directly to anyone who normally lives outside the UK.

You must deduct tax at the basic rate before making such payment and remit this tax to the Inland Revenue, unless otherwise agreed.

CLAIM FOR PERSONAL TAX ALLOWANCES FOR THE 1995/96 TAX YEAR

Every person resident in the UK is entitled to a personal allowance. The amount of your personal allowance depends on your age. You are granted a basic allowance if you were born after 5th April 1931.

From the 1995/96 tax year the married couples allowance, including the higher allowances for the over 65's, the widow's bereavement allowance and the additional personal allowance is given at the 15% rate only. These allowances are given at the 20% rate in 1994/95. So, for the 1995/96 tax year it is simpler to calculate your tax liability without reference to these allowances and then deduct from the tax payable 15% of the relevant allowance claimed.

Example:

Married couples allowance in 1995/96

A married man earns £15,000 a year. His liability for 1995/96 is as follows:

	£
Salary	15,000
Less Personal Allowance	3,525
Taxable	11,475
3,200 @ 20%	640
8,275 @ 25%	2,069
	2,709
Less Married Couples Allowance	
(1,720 @ 15%)	(258)
Tax Payable	2,451

ALLOWANCES FOR THOSE BORN BEFORE 6TH APRIL 1931

A higher personal allowance is available if you were born between the 6th April 1921 and the 5th April 1931. The highest personal allowance is available if you were born before the 6th April 1921.

ALLOWANCES TO BE CLAIMED BY MARRIED MEN

Married Couples Allowance

With the introduction of independent taxation on the 5th April 1990, a husband and wife are each:

- taxed on their own income
- given their own tax-free allowances
- given their own basic-rate bands
- responsible for their own tax affairs.

However, a married couple may claim an additional couple's allowance of £1,720 in the 1995/96 tax year. Higher married couple's allowances are available if either spouse is aged 65 or over or 75 or over in a particular tax year. A married couple's allowance is normally granted to the husband provided he is living with his wife, or separated but not divorced from his wife, and he pays her voluntary payments on which he does not get tax relief.

YEAR OF MARRIAGE

In the year of your marriage, you can claim the full married-couple's allowance if you married before the 6th May. If the wedding is on or after that date, your married-couple's allowance is reduced by one-twelfth for each complete month after the 6th April that you remained single.

Example:

Eric and Beth married on the 5th November 1995. Eric's salary for 1995/96 was £20,000. Beth's salary for 1995/96 was £18,000. Their income-tax liability is:

	1995/96	
	Eric	**Beth**
Salary	£20,000	£18,000
Personal Allowance	£3,525	£3,525
	£16,475	£14,475
Tax £3,200 @ 20%	£640	£640
TAX £13,275/£11,275 @ 25%	£3,319	£2,819
	£3,959	£3,459
Less Married Couple's Allowance £1,720 X 5/12 @ 15%	(£108)	-
Tax Payable	£3,851	£3,459

IF YOU OR YOUR WIFE WERE BORN BEFORE 6TH APRIL 1931

If you were entitled to the married couple's allowance and either you or your wife was born before 6th April 1931, you can claim a higher married couple's allowance. If you or your wife were born prior to 6th April 1921 you can claim the highest amount of married couple's allowance. Their higher allowances will be reduced by £1 for every £2 by which your total income, i.e. gross income less certain deductions e.g. mortgage interest etc. exceeds the income exemption limit (£14,200 in 1994/95 and £14,600 in 1995/96).

However, the allowance cannot be reduced below the amount of the basic married couple's allowance.

IF YOUR WIFE IS UNABLE TO LOOK AFTER HERSELF

An additional personal allowance for children applies to widows, widowers, single parents and others not entitled to the married persons allowance, £1,720 in the 1994/95 tax year. This allowance is also available if you are living with your wife, and she is totally incapacitated because of disability or illness and you have a child living with you.

MARRIED COUPLES

ALLOCATION OF MARRIED COUPLES ALLOWANCE

Prior to 5th Apri l 1993, the married couple's allowance automatically went to the husband. However, from 1993/94 onwards it is possible for married couples who are living together to elect for this allowance to be split between the two spouses or go entirely to the wife. However, you must make this election before the begining of the relevant tax year, i.e. an election for 1995/96 must be made before 6th April 1995. If this election is not made the allowance will go to the husband.

TRANSFER OF SURPLUS ALLOWANCES TO YOUR WIFE OR HUSBAND

If you are married and your allowances exceed your income, you may transfer your surplus allowances to your spouse, provided you live with your spouse during the tax year.

This allowance was introduced after the introduction of Independent Taxation in 1990/91. It was brought in to ensure that married couples were not worse off as a result of the introduction of Independent Taxation.

The amount transferred is known as the transitional allowance. To benefit from the transitional allowance in the 1994/95 tax year you must have been eligible for transitional allowance in 1990/91 and every tax year since then.

SPECIAL PERSONAL ALLOWANCE

You can claim this special allowance if you are a married man and you were claiming age related allowances in the 1989/90 tax year because your wife was over 65 in that year and you were not. This allowance ensures that married couples are not worse-off because of independent taxation. In the 1989/90 tax year, the level of a married man's age allowance depended on the greater of his own or his wife's age. After the introduction of independent taxation on 5th April 1990, the level of a married man's personal allowance depends on his age only. So, this special personal allowance ensures that you do not face a reduction in your allowances as a result of independent taxation. It is given if the husband's personal allowance and the married couple's allowance for 1990/91 together are less than the married age allowance you received for 1989/90.

If you are under 64 and your wife was aged 65 to 74 inclusive on the 5th April 1990, the special allowance is £3,400.

If you are under 75 and your wife was aged 75 or over on the 5th April 1990, the special allowance is £3,540.

This special allowance will be reduced by £1 for every £2 by which your total income i.e. gross income less certain deductions e.g. mortgage interest etc. exceeds the income exemption limit (£14,200 in 1994/95).

MARRIED WOMEN

Your husband is normally responsible for claiming the married couple's allowance and unless you write to your Inspector of Taxes, your husband will automatically receive this allowance. However, provided you are living with your husband, you may request that half of this allowance is given to you. Alternatively, both spouses may jointly request that the entire allowance be given to the wife. This request must be made prior to the commencement of the tax year.

WIDOWER

After the death of your wife, you continue to get the married couple's allowance for the rest of the tax year. You cannot get the additional personal allowance unless your wife was totally incapacitated and you have a dependent child.
In the following tax years, you get your personal allowance and any other allowances to which you are entitled e.g. an additional personal allowance if you have a dependent child.

WIDOWS

After the death of your husband, you get the part of the married couple's allowance which your husband had not used up to the date of his death, the widow's bereavement allowance, and an additional personal allowance if you have a dependent child.

In subsequent years, you get your personal allowance and any other allowances to which you are entitled, e.g. the additional personal allowance if you have a dependent child.

WIDOW'S BEREAVEMENT ALLOWANCE

Widow's bereavement allowance can be claimed in the tax year of your husband's death and in the following tax year, unless you remarry before that year begins. The allowance is £1,720 in the 1994/95 tax year. In 1994/95 this allowance is given at the lower rate of 20% and will be further restricted in 1995/96 to 15%.

If you are widowed, you do not qualify for widow's bereavement allowance in the year of your husband's death or additional personal allowance for dependent children, if you have already claimed a married couple's allowance.

Example:

Eric died in September 1995. His salary up to the date of death was £15,000. His widow Beth had income for 1995/96 of £9,000. After his death, she also received a private pension of £400 a month and a state pension of £2,500. In the 1995/96 tax year their position is as follows:

1995/96

	Eric		Beth
Salary	£15,000	Salary	£9,000
		Private Pension	£2,400
		State Pension	£2,500
		Total Income	£13,900
Personal Allowance	£3,525	Personal Allowance	£3,525
Taxable	£11,475	Taxable	£10,375
Tax Payable			
£3,200 @ 20%	£600	£3,200 @ 20%	£600
£8,275 @ 25%	£2,069 £2,669	£7,175 @ 25%	£1,793 £2,393
Less:		Less:	
Married Couple's Allowance £1,720 @ 15%	£258	Widow's Bereavement Allow. £1,720 @ 15%	£258
		Additional Personal Allow. £1,720 @ 15%	£258
	£2,411		£1,877

IF YOU HAVE A CHILD AND ARE SINGLE, SEPARATED, DIVORCED OR WIDOWED

This additional personal allowance may be claimed by widows/widowers and others such as single parents who are not entitled to married couple's allowance and people who have a dependent child. The amount of the allowance is equal to the married couple's allowance, £1,720 in the 1994/95 tax year.

If you have a dependent child, you may claim the additional personal allowance if you are:

- a single person
- a married woman who has separated from her husband
- a woman who marries during the tax year and has a dependent child before marriage
- a married man who is not entitled to the married couple's allowance because he is separated from his wife.

A dependent child is a child under 18 years of age at the begining of the tax year, whom you maintain at your own expense. Legally adopted, legitimate children and stepchildren are included. If the child is over 16 years of age, you may only claim the allowance if he/she is receiving full-time instruction at a university, college or school or is training full-time for at least two years for a trade or profession. The allowance is also given in respect of a child under 18 who is not your child but who is living with you and maintained by you.

If two more more people claim for the same child e.g. separated parents, the allowance may be split between them. If no agreement can be reached it will be split according to how much time the child lives with each of you. If you have more than one child, enter details of the youngest child.

If you are receiving half the married couple's allowance in the year of separation, you can also claim the additional personal allowance. However, the total of your share of the married couple's allowance and the additional personal allowance cannot exceed the amount of the married couple's allowance.

If a man was claiming an additional personal allowance before he got married, he can choose to keep it for the remainder of the tax year in which he gets married, instead of claiming the married couple's allowance.

If a woman was claiming an additional personal allowance before she got married, she can continue to claim it for the remainder of that tax year.

After the year of marriage, neither spouse can claim this additional allowance, unless the wife is totally incapacitated for the whole of the tax year. In that case, the husband can claim the allowance in addition to the married couple's allowance.

BLIND PERSON'S ALLOWANCE

A registered blind person is entitled to an extra personal allowance of £1,200. If you are unable to use the full amount of this allowance, the unused portion can be transferred to your spouse whether or not he/she is blind. A blind couple are each entitled to a separate blind person's allowance.

If you are a married person receiving this allowance and your allowances exceed your income, you may transfer any unused portion of this allowance to your spouse by completing Form 575.

Declaration

You should sign and date the return, and state the capacity in which you are acting in the case of executors, trustees etc. You should then enter your National Insurance Number and that of your wife, if it is not already shown on the front of the return.

A Worked Example: 1994/95

- William had a salary of £27,500 for the year ended 5th April 1995 and the use of a 1600 cc company car over four years old, its original market value was £9,000. He does 12,000 business miles p.a. William reimbursed his employer £100 for private use of the car. PAYE tax deducted £5,450 (P.60).

- Sarah, his wife, owns a Boutique and her adjusted profit for the year ended 31st December 1993 was £4,500. Wear and tear allowances amounted to £200 and she paid £300 Schedule D tax. William and Sarah are over 60, but under 65.

- William received two dividends from ICI in January 1995, amounting to £160 with tax credits of £40.

- For the year ended the 5th April 1993, Sarah received £150 deposit interest from the Midland Bank and William received £45 deposit interest with the Royal Bank of Scotland, after the deduction of retention tax.

- Sarah also received £200 gross interest from Government loan stock and £240 interest from her Building Society Share Account for the year ended 5th April 1993, after deduction of retention tax.

- Sarah has a life assurance policy costing £100 p.a. with Guardian Insurance, sum assured £40,000 (commencement date 01.06.83).

- Sarah paid £490 in medical insurance to BUPA in 1994.

- Sarah contributed £600 to a Personal Pension Plan.

- William paid £3,000 p.a. mortgage interest on his home loan of £28,000 - not under MIRAS.

Assessable Income - 1994/95

	William	Sarah
Salary	£27,500	-
B.I.K. Car & Petrol	£2,110	-
Boutique	-	£4,500
Dividends	£200	-
Interest - Midland Bank	-	£200
Interest - Royal Bank of Scotland	£60	-
Interest- Government Loan	-	£200
Interest - Building Society Interest	-	£320
Total Income	£29,870	£5,220

	William			Sarah	
Total Income		£29,870			£5,220
Deductions:					
Retirement Annuity		-			(£600)
Wear & Tear Allowance		-			(£200)
		£29,870			£4,420
Allowances					
Personal	£3,445			£3,445	
Medical Insurance	-			£490	
	-	£3,445		-	£3,935
Taxable		£26,425			£485

	Amount	Tax	Amount	Tax
Taxable at 20%	£3,000	£600	£485	£97
Taxable at 25%	£23,425	£5,856	-	-
Total Tax Payable	£23,425	£6456	£485	£97
Less: Married Couples				
Allow. £1,720 @ 20%		(£344)		
Less Mortgage Interest				
£3,000 @ 20%		(£600)		
		£5,512		

Tax Paid/Credit				
Dividends	£40			
Midland Bank	-		£50	
Royal Bank of Scotland	£15		-	
Building Society -	-		£80	
Tax Paid Sched. D.	-		£300	
Tax Paid PAYE.	£5,450			
Total Tax Paid/Credits		£5,505		£430
Bal. Due/(Overpaid)		£7		(£333)

Notes: Tax Credits are calculated @ 20% of gross investment income.

Life Insurance relief is granted at source at 12.5%, as the policy was taken out in 1983. Sarah will pay only £87.50 to the Insurance Company, which will in turn, claim £12.50 tax from the Inland Revenue.

Benefit in Kind is £9,000 @ 35%		£3,150
Less: 1/3 Reduction for mileage (1/3 of £3,150)		(£1,050)
Less: 1/3 for age of car (1/3 of £2,100)		(£700)
Less: amount re-imbursed		(£100)
Add Fuel Benefit		£810
Total Benefit in Kind		£2,110

TAX FORMS

During employment you will encounter some or all of the following tax forms.

- **P.45** When you commence new employment you give your new employer a copy of the P45 you received from the previous employer on termination of that employment.

- **P46** Your employer will give you P46 to complete when you start your first job.

- **P15** Coding claim - you complete a form P15 at the same time as form P46 and send it to the Inspector of Taxes to get a tax code.

- **P2T** This is your notice of coding which you will obtain from your Inspector of Taxes - it telsl you what your PAYE code is.

- **P38(s)** For students who get holiday jobs, if their total income doesn't exceed a personal allowance (£3,445 in the 1994/95 tax year).

- **P60** Your employer gives you a P60 at the end of each tax year - it tells you how much you've earned during that tax year and how much tax you have paid.

TAX RETURNS

There are several types of tax returns, designed for different taxpayers:

- **Form P1** This form is the simplest tax return and is normally reserved for employees whose tax affairs are uncomplicated or who earn less than £8,500 p.a. If Form P1 is the return which you complete, it is likely that you will be asked to keep your tax inspector informed of any new source of income.

- **Form 11P** This tax return is completed by most employees, when they are requested to do so by their inspector of taxes, normally every two/three years.

- **Form 11** This form is for self-employed people or people whose main sources of income are chargeable to tax under Schedule D.

- **Form R40** This form is similar to Form 11 and is normally completed by people who reclaim their tax each year.

- **Form R332** This form is used if you make a return on behalf of persons who cannot do so themsevles, e.g. children.

Inland Revenue

1994 Tax Return

| H M Inspector of Taxes | Date of issue | Tax reference | National Insurance number |

Tax Office address

What you must do with this form
You are required by law to:

- fill in this form

- sign the declaration on page 12

- send the form, and any documents asked for, back to me within 30 days.

If you don't and there is no good reason for sending this form in late, you may have to pay a penalty. You may also have to pay interest on any tax paid late because this form was not sent back in time. However, the Inland Revenue will not seek interest simply because of delay provided that the return is sent back by 31 October 1994 (or within 30 days of issue if it was sent to you after 2 October 1994). For further information please refer to the introduction in the enclosed leaflet *"Filling in your 1994 Tax Return"*, which you should use when completing the form

What details should you give ?
You only need to fill in the sections which apply to you and you may find that many of them do not apply to you.

You should show all the income and capital gains on which you may be charged to tax. Give details for the tax year which started on 6 April 1993 and ended on 5 April 1994 (1993-94) unless the form asks for something different.

You can also use this form to claim:

- expenses and deductions for 1993-94

- personal allowances for the tax year which started on 6 April 1994 and ends on 5 April 1995 (1994-95).

If there is not enough space for your entries please give details on a separate sheet of paper.

Do you need help ?
If you need help please contact your Tax Office. The address and telephone number are shown above. You will need to quote your tax reference and National Insurance number - *see above*. For general enquiries you may prefer to contact a Tax Enquiry Centre. Your local Tax Office (see under Inland Revenue in the phone book) can give you the address of your nearest one.

Notes

These notes give guidance and refer you to relevant parts in the leaflet "Filling in your 1994 Tax Return"

See note 2

Income from employment etc - year to 5 April 1994

Complete this section if you worked for an employer full-time, part-time or on a casual basis or for an agency. Also fill it in if you received director's fees or payments or benefits from any office you held.

If you have been given a form P60 by your employer, it should contain the information you need. Give your income before tax. If you are a director see notes 2 and 3. If you are not a director see notes 2 and 4

Wages, salary, fees, bonuses etc.
Your occupation and employer's name(s) and address(es)

£

Some of these are not liable to tax. See note 5

Lump sum and compensation payments
Give the amount of any lump sum or compensation payment you received during 1993-94, if this has not already been included in *Wages, salary, fees, bonuses etc* above.

£

Profit-related pay and profit sharing schemes

Give the number of profit-related pay schemes to which you belong

Tick here if you received a taxed sum from the trustees of an approved profit-sharing scheme.

Tick here if this sum is included under *Wages, salary, fees, bonuses etc* above.

11P (1994)

Other payments received

Give the amount and the type of work you did and the name(s) and address(es) of any employer(s) (if as overleaf, write 'As overleaf').

£

Business mileage is mileage necessarily travelled in the course of your work. It does not usually include mileage between home and work. See note 6.

Cars and car fuel

Tick here if you or a member of your family or household were provided with a car during the year because of your job and it was available for private use .

Tick the box corresponding with your business mileage in the car.

2,500 or less   2,501 to 17,999   18,000 or over

If you received car fuel for private travel in the car provided for you (or for a member of your family or household) tick the appropriate box.

petrol   diesel

For examples of the most common benefits see note 6.

Other benefits in kind and expenses allowances

List the benefits and give their values if you know them. List also types of expenses allowances made to you and give the total amounts. You can leave out altogether (in this item and in the next item) all amounts where the Inland Revenue has agreed with your employer through what is known as a 'dispensation' that the expenses are allowable and no tax will be payable .

£

See note 7.

Expenses for which you wish to claim a deduction

List here the types of expenses and give the amounts

£

Earnings from work abroad

Only complete this item if you wish to claim foreign earnings deduction.

If you were abroad for all, or nearly all, of a 365-day period, you may be able to claim a foreign earnings deduction of 100% (unless you were employed by the Crown). Ask for "Going to Work Abroad" (leaflet IR58). If you have paid foreign tax on your foreign earnings, you may be able to claim double taxation relief. See note 8.

If there is not enough space put the details on a separate sheet.

Your occupation abroad and employer's name and overseas address

Dates of period(s) spent abroad

| From | / | / 19 | to | / | / 19 | From | / | / 19 | to | / | / 19 |
| From | / | / 19 | to | / | / 19 | From | / | / 19 | to | / | / 19 |

Give the amount of your earnings in 1993-94 already included under one of the income items above which relate to the periods you have worked abroad.   £

Income from self-employment - year to 5 April 1994

Complete this section if you have income from self-employment. If you are in partnership give details for your share in the partnership only.

Details of your business

State what kind of self-employed work you do

See note 9 about keeping records. See note 10 about partnerships.

Business name, (and address if different from the address on page 1)

2

Notes .
*See note 11 and page 4
of this form.*
See notes 12 and 13.

*Ask for "Simple Tax
Accounts" (leaflet
IR104).*

Tick here if providing furnished accommodation in your only or main home amounts to a trade and you are in the *Rent-a Room* scheme.

Businesses with a turnover of less than £15,000
If you were in business on your own, or in partnership, and your turnover (or the partnership's turnover) was less than £15,000 a year you do not need to send accounts. You may, instead, give details of turnover and allowable business expenses.

Turnover £   Allowable business expenses £

*See notes 13 for
expenses. See note 14
for losses.*

All businesses: Profit for tax purposes
Your profit for tax purposes is your turnover less allowable business expenses. It does not include enterprise allowance received. Give your profit for the accounting period you specify below. If you have made a loss enter 'Nil'. £

Accounts
If your turnover was £15,000 or more, you should return this form with a statement of your profit or loss for tax purposes supported by full accounts. You should also do this if your turnover was less than £15,000 and you choose not to enter your turnover and expenses above.

Period covered by your accounts or statement of turnover and expenses
Give the period covered by your accounts (or the partnership accounts), or by the statement of turnover and expenses above, which ended on a date between 6 April 1993 and 5 April 1994. If you stopped being self-employed, give the date you stopped.

Start of period   / / 19   End of period   / / 19

Capital allowances
Give the amount you are claiming or tick here and give details on a separate sheet of paper if you want your Tax Office to help work out the figure. £

Balancing adjustments
Give the amount of the adjustment or tick here and give details on a separate sheet of paper if you want your Tax Office to help work out the figure. £

Enterprise allowance received £

Further relief on Class 4 National Insurance

Type of relief   Amount
   £

Income from Pensions and Superannuation - year to 5 April 1994

*If you want more
information ask for
"Income Tax and
Pensioners" (leaflet
IR121).
See note 20 for what
counts as a pension.*

Complete this section if you received or were entitled to a pension in 1993-94.
State Pensions
Give the full amount you were entitled to in 1993-94. If you are a married man enter only the amount payable to you. If you are a married woman you should enter the pension payable to you, even if it was paid to you as a result of your husband's contributions. Include widows pension here but include widowed mother's allowance under *Other Social Security benefits* overleaf. £

Other Pensions
*You should find the
information you need
on the form P60 which
the payer should have
given you after the end
of the tax year, or any
other certificate of
pension paid and tax
deducted. See note 8 if
your pension is from
abroad.*
Include:
• pensions from a former employer (paid either in the UK or abroad)
• pensions you receive from your late husband's/wife's former employer (paid either in the UK or abroad)
• pensions from a personal pension plan or retirement annuity contract
• pensions from Free Standing Additional Voluntary Contribution Schemes
• pensions for injuries at work or for work-related illness
• other pensions from abroad
• pensions from service in the armed forces.
Do **not** include war widows' pensions and pensions for wounds or disability in military service or for other war injuries as these are not taxable.

Give the name(s) and address(es) of the payer(s) of the pension and the full amount of your pension(s) for 1993-94.

*If there is not enough
space put the details on
a separate sheet of
paper.*

£

Surpluses repaid from a Free Standing Additional Voluntary Contributions scheme
Complete this item if, when you retired or left pensionable service, some of your contributions from a free-standing additional voluntary contributions (FSAVC) scheme were repaid to you. **Give the gross amount** shown on the certificate given to you by the scheme administrator. £

206

This section asks for pension(s) information for the year ending on 5 April 1995.
The pension section on the previous page asked you for details about your pension(s) for the year which ended on 5 April 1994.

See note 20 for what counts as a state pension

Income from pensions - year to 5 April 1995

If you currently receive a pension or expect to start receiving a pension before 6 April 1995, please give the details asked for below. In the column headed "Amount of pension you receive or expect to receive", please show:

• for pensions you already receive - the amount you get at the time you fill the form in

• for pensions you expect to start receiving - the amount you will get (if you know it).

Starting date (if after 5 April 1994)	Amount of pension you receive or expect to receive .	Say whether this is per week, every 4 weeks, each month, every 3 months or per year	Tick if this is after tax	Tick if a state pension
/ /19	£			
/ /19	£			
/ /19	£			
/ /19	£			
/ /19	£			

Income from National Insurance and Social Security benefits - year to 5 April 1994

If you claimed unemployment benefit or income support because you were unemployed during 1993-94 give the name of your benefit office

Other Social Security benefits

If you claimed any of these benefits, give the full amount you were entitled to in 1993-94.

Widowed mother's allowance	£
Invalid care allowance	£
Industrial death benefit	£

Income from property - year to 5 April 1994

Complete this section if you receive income from letting property in the UK or abroad. If you let more than one property give details for each property separately.

Furnished rooms in your only or main home (UK homes only)

Under the Rent-a-Room scheme the first £3,250 of gross income from furnished rooms in your only or main home can be tax-free. You may not then claim any expenses or capital allowances. Alternatively, you can choose not to take part in the scheme and instead declare all the income and claim expenses and capital allowances in the normal way.

The tax-free amount is reduced to £1,625 if someone else is also letting furnished rooms in your home.

Tick one of the three boxes below if you let furnished rooms in your only or main home:

1 Your gross income **plus** any balancing charge was no more than £3,250 (or if appropriate £1,625) and you do not opt out of the scheme.

You do not need to give any more details.

2 Your gross income **excluding** any balancing charge was more than £3,250 (or if appropriate £1,625) and you want to be assessed on the difference between the rents and this tax-free amount, with no claim for expenses or capital allowances.

Show:

• Gross income (excluding any balancing charge) | £

• Tax-free amount (£3,250 if you are the only person letting furnished rooms in your home or £1,625 if someone else is letting furnished rooms in your home). | £

• Balancing charge (if any) | £

If the income is from a furnished holiday letting enter 'Holiday letting'.

3 Neither box 1 nor box 2 applies. Your rental income, expenses and capital allowances will be treated in the normal way. Give details under *Other rentals in the UK* on page 5 unless the lettings amount to a trade. In this case give details under *Income from self-employment* on pages 2 and 3.

4

Other rentals in the UK

Address of the property you let

Tick to show the type of rental

Furnished holiday letting

Furnished property

Unfurnished property

Ground rents and feu duties

Land

Include rent paid in kind and profits from supplying gas or electricity but not premiums. For expenses see note 24.

Gross rents due and other income received in 1993-94   £

Expenses   £

Gross income less expenses   £

If your gross rents etc before expenses were £15,000 or more enclose a detailed statement for each property of how you reached your figure for expenses.

Premiums received   £

Length of lease if you received a premium   £

Your Tax Office will work out how much of the premium is income and how much is capital gains.

Property abroad

Address, including country, of the property you let

Gross rents due and other income received in 1993-94   £

Expenses   £

Gross income less expenses   £

Income from savings and investments - year to 5 April 1994

See note 26 for income you do not need to include. If you have joint savings and investments see note 27.

Complete this section if you received any interest, dividends from shares, income from unit trusts or other investment income. Even if the income was reinvested (ie not actually paid out to you) you must still give details. **If you received income from a jointly owned investment or a joint savings account, give only your share of the income.**

The first £70 of interest on National Savings Ordinary Accounts is exempt from tax, but must still be included here.

National Savings

Give the amounts you received, as shown on your statement. In the case of Capital Bonds, give the interest added to the Capital Bonds, as shown on your statement.

Ordinary Account	£
Investment Account	£
Deposit Bonds	£
Income Bonds	£
Capital Bonds	£

First Option Bonds

Give the amount you received as shown on your tax certificate

Net interest after tax	Tax deducted	Gross interest before tax
£	£	£
£	£	£
£	£	£

Your bank or building society should be able to supply the details you need, but see note 28.

Do not forget to include interest from current accounts and accounts closed during the year.

Income from other UK banks, building societies and deposit takers

Name of the bank, building society, savings bank or deposit taker. Tick box if you have registered to have interest paid gross	Interest after tax (leave blank if no tax was deducted)	Tax deducted (leave blank if no tax was deducted)	Gross interest
	£	£	£
	£	£	£
	£	£	£
	£	£	£
	£	£	£
	£	£	£

Include interest on Government stocks (gilts), bonds, loans to individuals etc. See note 29.

Other interest you receive in the UK

Give the source of the interest	Interest after tax (leave blank if no tax was deducted)	Tax deducted (leave blank if no tax was deducted)	Gross interest
	£	£	£
	£	£	£
	£	£	£

5

Dividends from shares in UK companies
Do not include income from trusts, loan stock, dividends from overseas companies or stock dividends.

Name of the company	Tax credit	Dividend
	£	£
	£	£
	£	£
	£	£

Stock dividends
If you took up an offer of shares in place of a cash dividend (a 'stock dividend'), give the "appropriate amount in cash" notified by the company in the dividend column.

Name of the company	Notional tax credit	Dividend
	£	£
	£	£
	£	£
	£	£

Income from UK unit trusts
Complete this if you received income from unit trusts, including income reinvested in units. If your voucher shows a tax credit, give the tax credit and the dividend. If your voucher shows tax deducted, give the tax deducted and the gross income.

Give the name of each unit trust	Tax credit or tax deducted	Dividend	Gross income
	£	£	£
	£	£	£
	£	£	£
	£	£	£

Accrued income, charges and allowances
Give details of the transactions and enter the charges and allowances for the year.

	Charges
	£

	Allowances
	£

Income from savings and investments abroad

Describe the source and state the country	Foreign tax deducted	UK tax deducted	Gross income
	£	£	£
	£	£	£
	£	£	£
	£	£	£

Other income from savings and investments

For company distributions give the tax credit, if any, and distribution. For all other income give the tax deducted, if any, and the gross income.

Describe the source	Distribution	Tax credit or tax deducted	Gross income
	£	£	£
	£	£	£
	£	£	£
	£	£	£

Other income - year to 5 April 1994

Income from trusts funded by others
Complete this item if you received or were entitled to receive income from a trust set up by someone else.

Name of trust

Tick here if any income was taxed at 20% (or carried a 20% tax credit) £

Tick here if the income is from a discretionary/accumulation trust

Income and capital from settlements for which you have provided funds
Complete this item if the income, or payments of capital, should be treated as belonging to you for tax purposes.

Name and/or brief details of the settlement

Tick here if any income was taxed at 20% (or carried a 20% tax credit) £

Income from estates
Complete this item if you had a legal entitlement to income from the estate of someone who has died but whose estate was under administration. If the personal representative of the estate has given you an income tax certificate, give the amount of gross income shown on the certificate.

Name of deceased person	Nature of your entitlement to the estate	
		£

6

Notes

Maintenance and alimony you receive

Complete this item if you receive maintenance or alimony payments under:

- a legally enforceable agreement first made before 15 March 1988 and received by a Tax Office by 30 June 1988 or
- court order first made before 15 March 1988, or by 30 June 1988 if the application to the court was made before 16 March 1988 or
- a court order or legal agreement or Child Support Assessment which replaces, varies or adds to such an order or agreement.

Date the original order or agreement was first made   /   / 19

If there is not enough space, attach a separate sheet of paper

Date of any further order, agreement, or Child Support Assessment, if original order or agreement has been amended, or replaced or added to since 15 March 1988.   /   / 19

Up to £1,720 may be exempt from tax. See note 36. Ask for "Separation, divorce and maintenance payments" (IR93).

Amount received in 1993-94   £

Tick here if you wish to claim exemption from tax for maintenance or alimony received.

See note 37.

All other income or profits

Give sources and amounts of any other income etc which is taxable as yours and which you have not entered elsewhere on this form.

£

Mortgage or loan for main home

See note 38. Do not include interest on overdrafts or credit cards, or home improvement loans taken out after 5 April 1988.

Complete this section if you paid interest in 1993-94 on a mortgage or other loan to buy your main home in the UK. Also complete this section if you paid interest on a loan which you took out before 6 April 1988 to:

- improve your main home or
- buy or improve the main home of your divorced or separated husband/wife or of certain relatives.

See note 39.

Joint mortgages with someone who is not your husband/wife
Tick here and give details below only for your share of the mortgage.

If you had more than one loan during the year, for example if you moved and paid off a loan, give details of all loans. (On a separate sheet of paper if necessary)

Husband and wife: change in interest relief split
If you are married and you and your husband/wife want to change the way mortgage interest relief is split between you, tick here and you will be sent a form on which you can do this.

Details of loan
Give details of each advance or loan separately. If the loan is not from a building society and you do not have mortgage interest relief at source enclose a form MIRAS 5, or other certificate of interest paid from your lender.

Name of lender

Account number

Tick here if not in MIRAS

Date loan started
if after 6 April 1993   /   /19

If you paid off the loan during the year
Address of the property

Date loan paid off   /   / 19

Notes

For details of loans on which you can claim tax relief see note 40. For details on loans to buy or improve rental property see notes 24 and 25. If you have more than one qualifying loan, give details on a separate sheet of paper.

Other qualifying loans

Complete this if you can claim tax relief on other loans. Only give details of loans not included elsewhere on this form. Enclose a certificate of interest paid from your lender. Do not include loans on your main home.

Name of lender

Purpose of loan

Give the address of the property if the loan is for the purchase or improvement of property used for letting.

The number of weeks let

Amount of gross interest paid in the 1993-94 tax year

£

Pension contributions etc

You may be able to claim certain payments as a deduction from your earned income. See notes 41, 43 and 44. If you only pay into your employer's occupational pension and/or AVC scheme, you do not need to fill in this section.

Complete this section if you made payments to retirement annuities, personal pension contracts, freestanding additional voluntary contribution schemes (FSAVC), or trade union or friendly society death benefit and superannuation schemes.

Retirement annuity payments
Name of retirement annuity provider

Contract or membership number

Amount paid in 1993-94

£

If your payments altered during 1993-94 enclose the original payment receipts or statement of revised payments from your retirement annuity provider.

Tick here if you want to deduct all or part of the payments you made in 1993-94 from your profits or earnings from an earlier tax year. You will be sent a separate form to make your claim.

Amount you expect to pay in 1994-95

£

Personal pension contributions
Name of personal pension provider

Basic rate tax relief on personal pension contributions made by employees is given at source.

Contract or membership number

Amount paid in 1993-94

£

Tick here if you want to deduct all or part of the pension contributions you made in 1993-94 from your profits or earnings from an earlier tax year.
You will be sent a separate form to make your claim.

See note 42.
You cannot deduct employer's contributions from earnings from an earlier tax year.

Amount contributed by your employer in 1993-94

£

If this is your first claim, enclose the original contribution certificate (PPCC) from your pension provider. If your payments have altered during 1993-94, enclose original payment receipts or any original supplementary form PPCC.

Amount you expect to pay in 1994-95 (if you know it)

£

Amount your employer expects to contribute in the 1994-95 tax year (if you know it)

£

Trade union or friendly society death benefit and superannuation schemes
Name of the trade union or friendly society or scheme

Total amount paid in 1993-94

£

Amount relating to death or superannuation benefits

£

Note 63 lists the
amounts of the personal
tax allowances for
1994-95.

Claim for personal tax allowances for year to 5 April 1995

A personal tax allowance is not a payment to you. It reduces the amount of tax you have to pay. **You will be given the basic personal allowance automatically** each tax year if you are resident in the UK. Use this section to claim any other or higher allowances to which you are entitled.

See note 55

Allowances for those born before 6 April 1930

You may be able to claim a higher amount of personal allowance if you were born before 6 April 1930.

Tick here to make your claim.

Allowances to be claimed by married men.

You can only claim if
you can tick one of
these two boxes.

Married couple's allowance
Tick the relevant box to claim

Give your wife's full name

See note 56

You are living with your wife.

You separated from your wife before 6 April 1990 but are still married to her and have wholly maintained her since the separation with voluntary payments for which you are not entitled to any tax relief.

If you married after 5 April 1993 give the date of your marriage

/ / 19

See note 55

If you or your wife were born before 6 April 1930
If you are entitled to the married couple's allowance, you can claim a higher amount of allowance if you or your wife were born before 6 April 1930.

Tick here to make your claim.

If your wife was born before 6 April 1930, give her date of birth

/ / 19

See note 59

If your wife is unable to look after herself
You may be able to claim the additional personal allowance if
* you are living with your wife who is totally incapacitated because of disability or illness
* **and** you have a child living with you.

Give the child's date of birth

/ / 19

Give your wife's illness or disability

Tick here if the child lives with you.

Tick here if your wife is likely to be unable to look after herself throughout the tax year ending on 5 April 1995.

If the child was 16 or over on 6 April 1994 and in full-time education or training give the name of the university, college or school; or the type of training.

Give the name of the youngest child for whom you can claim.

Married couples

Allocation of married couple's allowance

See note 57

A husband is responsible for claiming the married couple's allowance, but if you are living together you may choose how the allowance is to be allocated between you.
For 1995-96 you can jointly ask for the whole of the allowance to be given to one of you.
Or, either of you can ask for half of the allowance and it will then be divided equally between you.

Tick here if you wish to do this and you will be sent a form.
(You do not have to complete a form if you want the allocation for 1994-95 to continue in 1995-96).

Transfer of surplus allowances to your wife or husband

Ask your Tax Office
for A Guide for
Married Couples
(leaflet IR80).
See note 62 for blind
person's allowance.

To transfer any surplus allowances you must have been married and living with your wife or husband at any time in 1994-95. If you did not have enough income tax liability to use all (or any) of your married couple's allowance then you may transfer the surplus to your wife or husband.

Tick here if you need a transfer notice form.

If you have insufficient income to use all (or any) blind person's allowance you are entitled to then you may transfer any surplus to your wife or husband. If you are a husband who does not have sufficient income to use his personal allowance in some circumstances your wife may receive transitional allowance.

See note 58

Allowance for widows
You may be able to claim this allowance for the tax year in which your husband died and also the following year.

Give the date of your husband's death

Tick here to make your claim

/ / 19

Notes

If you have a child and are single, separated, divorced or widowed

See notes 59 and 60.

You may be able to claim the additional personal allowance if you have a child living with you for at least part of the year and you are single, separated, divorced or widowed at some time during the year.

Give the child's date of birth   /   / 19

Give the name of the youngest child for whom you can claim

If the child was 16 or over on 6 April 1994 and in full-time education or training give the name of the university, college or school or the type of training.

Tick here if the child lives with you.

Shared claims

See note 61.

Complete this item if:
- another person is claiming for the child named above or
- you live together as husband and wife with another person, but you are not married to him/her, and that person is also entitled to claim this allowance.

Tick here if you want the allowance to be shared equally between you.

If you do not want the allowance to be shared equally, state how you want it to be shared

Give the other person's (or your partner's) name and address

If you do not live with the other person and you cannot agree how you want the allowance shared between you, give the number of days in the tax year that the child lives with you and the number of days the child lives with the other person.

Blind person's allowance

Note 62 has details.

Tick here to claim the allowance.

Give the name of the Local Authority or equivalent body with which you have registered your blindness.

Give the date you registered   /   / 19

Personal details

National Insurance number If different from the one shown on the front of this form

If you are a serving member of H M Forces give your rank.

Change of address. If you no longer live at the address shown on the front of this form, give your current address.

Date of birth (if you were born before 6 April 1935 or are paying self-employed pension contributions)

Marital status. State if you are single, married, widowed, separated or divorced.

You do not have to, but if you wish you can give your day time telephone number so that we can contact you if we have any queries.

Declaration

Before you send your completed form back to your Tax Office, **you must sign the statement below.** If you give false information or conceal any part of your income or chargeable gains, you can be prosecuted.

You should keep a copy of your completed form or make entries in the boxes in the leaflet "Filling in your 1994 Tax Return".

The information I have given on this form is correct and complete to the best of my knowledge and belief.

Signature

Date   /   / 19

If signing for someone else

If you are signing this form on behalf of someone else give the following details:

Your name and your private address

Name of the person for whom you are signing

The capacity in which you are signing, for example, as executor, trustee, receiver, factor etc.

Postcode

12

Notes

FSAVC schemes

Complete this item if you pay into a free-standing additional voluntary contribution (FSAVC) and you wish to claim higher rate tax relief. Give the amount you paid this year before your FSAVC scheme claimed any tax refund.

Name of FSAVC provider

Contract or membership number

Amount paid in 1993-94 £

If this is your first claim, enclose the original contribution certificate (VCC) which your FSAVC provider should have sent you. If your payments have altered during 1993-94, enclose original payment receipts from your FSAVC provider.

Amount you expect to pay in 1994-95 (if you know it) £

Other deductions

Do not give details of maintenance or alimony payments which cannot be legally enforced.

Maintenance or alimony payments

Fill in this item if you make payments to maintain your children or divorced or separated husband/wife under a court order, decree of the court, a legally binding agreement or Child Support Assessment.

The rules for tax relief depend on the date of the first order or agreement. Your Tax Office will work out the amount you can claim. See note 48.

Date of your current order, agreement or Child Support Assessment / / 19
If your current order , agreement or Child Support Assessment is dated on or after 15 March 1988 and varies, replaces or revives an earlier order or agreement which was in force on 15 March 1988 give the date of that earlier order. / / 19

Amount you were ordered to pay in 1993-94 £

Amount you actually paid in 1993-94 (if this is different from the amount given above) £

Name(s) of person(s) you paid

Tick here if the payments are to your ex-husband/wife and he/she has remarried.

Give the date of remarriage if you know it. / / 19

Payments of this type may be partly tax deductible in 1993-94 and later years.

If you made payments to the Department of Social Security to cover Income Support for your separated or divorced wife/husband or for the maintenance by her/him of children of the marriage under a Court Order, or Child Support Assessment, show the amount you paid in 1993-94 . £

Tick here if you will be making payments of this kind in 1994-95.

If you would like more details ask your Tax Office for "Tax Relief for Private Medical Insurance" (leaflet IR103).

Private medical insurance for people aged 60 or over

Complete this if you paid private medical insurance premiums for someone aged 60 or over (including you and/or your husband/wife) under a contract that was eligible for tax relief. If you wish to claim tax relief at the higher rate, please ask your insurer for a certificate of premiums paid in 1993-94 and then send it to your Tax Office.

See note 46. Basic rate relief is given at source: give the amount you actually paid.

Name of insurer

Contract number   **Net amount paid in 1993-94** £

If you made "Gift Aid" donations give the amounts you actually paid to each charity. Use a separate sheet of paper if necessary.

Gift aid donations

Name of charity

Net amount paid in 1993-94 £

Covenants to charity

Give the amounts you actually paid to each charity. Use a separate sheet of paper if necessary. See note 47.

Name of charity

Net amount paid in 1993-94 £

Other covenants, bonds of annuity and settlements etc

Do not include most covenants made after 14 March 1988. See note 47.

Name of the person you pay   Date(s) of the deed(s)   **Gross amount paid in 1993-94** £

Vocational training

Name of training organisation

Net amount paid in 1993-94 for training that qualifies for tax relief.

£

Complete this section if you have sold or given away any assets which are subject to capital gains tax, or in any other way made gains subject to Capital Gains Tax in 1993-94.

To find out if you are liable, see notes 49 and 50. See note 50 for reliefs.

See notes 51 and 52 for information about calculating capital gains.

Capital gains - year to 5 April 1994

Tick here if the total value of any **assets** you have disposed of in 1993-94 was £11,600 or less and your chargeable gains were £5,800 or less. You do not then need to give any further details.

If the total value of the assets you disposed of in 1993-94 was more than £11,600 and/or the chargeable gains you made were more than £5,800, you must give details of the gain on each asset separately. If there is not enough room on this form give details on a separate sheet of paper.

Chargeable assets disposed of

Describe the asset and give the amount of chargeable gain

£

Total chargeable gains (before annual exemption) £

Chargeable gains from other sources

Complete this item if you have made gains which became subject to tax in 1993-94 but are not gains from the disposal of chargeable assets in 1993-94 or gains dealt with in the next two sections, *"If you benefit from a non-resident or dual resident settlement"* and, *"If you are the settlor of a settlement."*

Date gains became subject to tax / / 19

Reason gains became subject to tax

Gains accruing in 1993-94 £

If you benefit from a non-resident or dual resident settlement
Name of the settlement

Inland Revenue reference

Value of any cash payment, loan, asset or other benefit received from the settlement not subject to income tax. £

Date received / / 19

If you are the settlor of a settlement
Name of settlement

Inland Revenue reference

Amount of any chargeable gains by reference to which you, as settlor, are chargeable. £

Payments abroad

Give the gross amounts of any payments of rent on UK property or yearly interest which you make to someone who normally lives outside the UK. £

Tick here if you would like to be sent further details of how much tax you should deduct before making payments.

INDEX